THE STARS AND THE STILLNESS

A Portrait of George MacDonald

Kathy Triggs

The lightning and thunder,
They go and they come;
But the stars and the stillness
Are always at home.

Lutterworth Press · Cambridge

British Library Cataloguing in Publication Data

Triggs, Kathy
 The stars and the stillness : a portrait of
 George MacDonald.
 1. MacDonald, George, *1824–1905*—Biography
 2. Authors, Scottish—19th century—Biography
 I. Title
 823'.8   PR4968

 ISBN 0–7188–2625–0

First published 1986

Lutterworth Press
7 All Saints' Passage
Cambridge CB2 3LS

Photoset and printed in Great Britain by
Redwood Burn Limited,
Trowbridge, Wiltshire

Contents

List of Illustrations

Introduction

During his lifetime George MacDonald enjoyed great prestige and was extremely influential. As a writer and thinker his contemporaries ranked him with Trollope, Tennyson and Carlyle. Sir William Geddes wrote: 'In native gift of poetic insight he was born with a richer dower than has fallen to any of our age now living since Alfred Tennyson saw the light of day.'[1] Yet today his work is largely neglected. Those with a taste for fairy tales may enjoy his book *The Princess and the Goblin* and its sequel *The Princess and Curdie*, which are still in print, but the bulk of his work is out of print and hard to obtain.

The reasons for MacDonald's decline in popularity are not hard to find. He was essentially a Christian thinker, writing at a time when the reading public thought of itself as Christian. The twentieth century has seen a general decline in religious faith, and has felt that George MacDonald has little of value to offer. Another factor has been the busier life-style of the twentieth century. Victorian readers had plenty of time to consume bulky volumes, whose very weight seemed to promise spiritual nourishment. A hundred years later the reader wants a shorter, less demanding book; above all, he wants to be entertained. MacDonald appeals to his own time. He is not an easy read, though well worth a little trouble. In his novels passages of brilliant writing are often interrupted with mini-sermons, which spoil the effect for some readers. MacDonald made his points with great emphasis, perhaps unnecessarily. It may be that his novels could appeal to modern readers in an abridged form. (Some abridgements have been published in the USA.)

It may be, also, that MacDonald has something of ethical value to offer modern readers. The late twentieth century is seeing a revival of fundamentalist Christian attitudes and a resurgence of 'Victorian' approval of self-help, self-interest and self-righteousness. Society seeks the security of undeviating rules for conduct and belief. MacDonald offers an alternative—more risky, perhaps, but more satisfying. In his life and works he demonstrates the power and effectiveness of conduct and beliefs based not on rules but on the flexible interplay of personal relationships. And in this he includes both God and his neighbour.

MacDonald is a symbolist *par excellence*. He is able to express universal truths in terms of things that are common to every man in every age. Light and darkness, childhood and old age are such symbols. Stairs and stairways are a recurring image in MacDonald's works, as are windows and mirrors. Fire, water and wind are also significant images for him. In fact, the whole of nature is for him an expression of the spiritual realm that lies beyond it. The world is an incarnation—an expression in material terms—of its Father–Creator.

MacDonald's life covered three-quarters of the nineteenth century. A study of his life and works is in effect a study of the Victorian period. He was in touch with many of the movements of his time. He had contact with the Christian Socialists, with advocates for women's emancipation, with the higher ranks of government, and with the literary world. As this list implies, he was in some things a rebel within the establishment camp. He cared passionately for the plight of the poor and for better education for women and children; he helped by his writing to arouse concern in others. He was above all a rebel in the sphere of religion. He hated the atmosphere of cant and hypocrisy that characterised the nineteenth century, and campaigned against it. He was counted by some a heretic for his opposition to formalised, dogmatic religion; on the other hand for many of his readers he opened the windows and let in the wind of heaven.

He was particularly opposed to the vicious strife that prevailed among the religious denominations of his day. In England, members of the established church (the Church of England or Anglican Church) enjoyed social and political privileges denied to the Nonconformist or Dissenting churches. A 'Church' tradesman, for example, was higher in the social scale than a dissenting tradesman, all other things being equal. Dissenters were not admitted to the universities for many years; students had to subscribe to the Thirty-Nine Articles of the Church of England before taking a degree. Nor were they allowed to enter politics; all MPs had to be Anglicans. The dissenters replied with a sort of inverted snobbery. The religious periodicals of the nineteenth century are, at their worst, a catalogue of invective and diatribe, using God, the Bible and religion to prove that 'We are right; all others are wrong.' In Scotland, where MacDonald was brought up, things were a little different. The established church, which was Presbyterian, was of less importance because Scotland was ruled from Westminster. The Scottish universities were open to undergraduates of any denomination. Religious differences, however, were pursued with just as much fervour and bitterness as in England.

Into such an environment MacDonald brought a ray of light. Beginning as a Congregationalist, he ended his life as a member of the Anglican Church. He had to belong to a particular denomination or separate himself entirely from his fellow-Christians; but he refused to support any party factions. He was in sympathy with theologians of such opposing views as F. D. Maurice and C. H. Spurgeon. He cared more about the individual's relationship with God than pernickety theological arguments. He tried to set men's feet on the path of righteousness. Obey the will of God, he urged; then you will learn from Him, and the Truth will be yours.

It is typical of him that no 'school' of thought is associated with his name. Such an idea was anathema to him. He was the best of teachers in that he pointed beyond himself and encouraged his students to think for themselves. He knew that the essence of the faith cannot be learned at second-hand; as he said,

> Me, the schools, yourselves forsake;
> In your souls a silence make;
> Hearken till a whisper come,
> Listen, follow, and be dumb.[2]

His works cannot be formed into a system; rather, what he says must be made a part of the reader. Then it may be reproduced in his own work. C. S. Lewis is a prime example of this.

He said that everything he wrote owed its origin to George MacDonald.

Although he refused to make himself an idol, MacDonald did not try to keep himself to himself. On the contrary, he included many biographical details in his books. He drew on family and friends for characters, and included many of his own experiences as well as places he had visited or lived in. These are, of course, fictionalised; only a biography can express the shape and meaning of MacDonald's whole life.

In the early years of this century a 'Critical Appreciation' of MacDonald was written by Joseph Johnson, who knew many of MacDonald's friends in the Manchester area. It was published in 1906, shortly after the novelist's death. It seems that Johnson hurried to get his book printed as a memorial to his hero. That Johnson admired MacDonald is obvious in the uncritical, adulatory praises he heaped upon him. But the book contains many mistakes, and cannot be relied on for accuracy.

MacDonald's son Ronald wrote a reminiscence of his father in *From a Northern Window*, published in 1911. Entitled 'George MacDonald: A Personal Note', it includes many interesting details about the man himself.

In 1924, the centenary of the writer's birth, his eldest son Greville MacDonald published a biography with the title *George MacDonald and his Wife*. In its introduction he remarked that 'George MacDonald had expressed a hope that his Life would not be written: his message was all in his books, and no biography could add to it.'[3] However, in view of the imperfections of Johnson's book, Greville felt that he should undertake to give a more objective—and factually correct—picture of his father and mother.

Eight years later, in 1932, he produced his own memoirs, *Reminiscences of a Specialist*, which included many more personal details of his relationship with his mother and father. All four books have been long out of print, though *George MacDonald and his Wife*, and Joseph Johnson's *George MacDonald—A Biographical and Critical Appreciation* have recently been reissued in the United States.

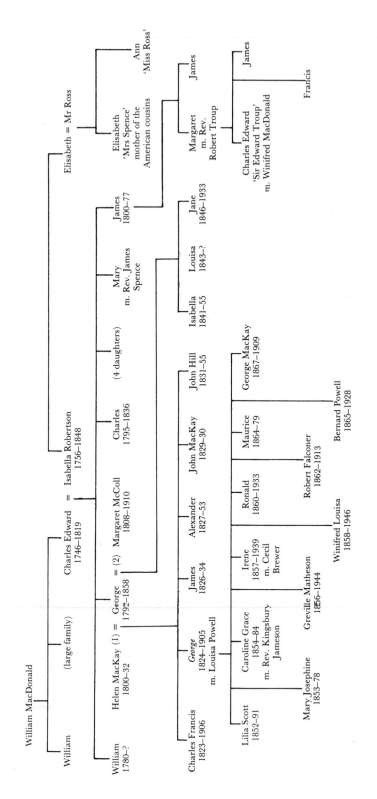

The family of George MacDonald

Reads from the back row, left to right:

Winifred	Lilia	Louisa	Irene	Ted Hughes
	Grace	George M	Mackay	Mary
Ronald	Robert	Greville	Bernard	
	Maurice			

Picture 1. The George MacDonald family in 1876, the year before the move to Italy. The group includes Mary's fiancé, Ted Hughes. This may have been the last complete family gathering. Mary and Maurice were to die within three years. (*Photo: MacDonald-Troup Collection*)

Picture 2. The Farm, Huntly. George MacDonald lived here from the ages of two to fifteen. His uncle, aunt and cousins shared the accommodation with his own family. (*Photo: Graham Webster*)

I

Huntly 1824–40

George MacDonald's birthplace, Huntly in Aberdeenshire, was of immense importance to his future development. He spent the whole of his childhood in this neat little town in the Scottish hills, gaining an intimate knowledge of the area through games and exploits with his brothers and friends. His father was a tenant of the Duke of Gordon. For many years the Gordons had held sway in this part of Scotland, and most of the people George knew—that is to say, most of the inhabitants of Huntly—were clansmen or tenants of the Gordons. Hence the Gordon influence was pervasive in Huntly. Its chief hotel was The Gordon Arms, and on the perimeter of the town, to the north, at the confluence of the Rivers Bogie and Deveron, stood the ruins of Huntly Castle, once the residence of the eldest son of the Duke of Gordon, the Marquess of Huntly.

George knew the ruins well: they were a favourite haunt of his. With his brothers, Charles, James, Alec and John, he had climbed over every inch. At the top of its great towers he could pretend to be the second Marquess in the Civil War, on the lookout for his enemy General Monro leading the Army of the Covenant to besiege Huntly Castle. Or down in the dungeons the boys could hark back to an even earlier period, when the clans flourished and every member of another clan might be an enemy. They knew the story of how one of the Gordons particularly merited the hatred of his foes by his inhumane treatment of his captives. He used to keep in the dungeon the orphaned children of those he had slain in battle, and have them driven up to feed from pigtroughs in the castle yard, to provide entertainment for himself and his retainers. The Mac-

1

Donald boys could go up and down the very stairway which led from the dungeons.

The Castle had been unoccupied since the Civil War, but its Lodge, half a mile to the north, was refurbished in 1747 by the third Duke. In George's boyhood the Lodge was inhabited by the Duchess of Gordon, the saintly widow of the fourth Duke. Her husband died in 1827, and George MacDonald's 'earliest definable memory',[1] as he called it when he recorded it in later life, was of the Duke's funeral cortège travelling from London through Huntly to the family burial-place at Elgin. At two and a half years of age the little boy watched the procession, silent save for the horses' hoofs and the rumbling wheels on the cobblestones: black horses with nodding black plumes, and black carriages draped in black velvet.

This early memory epitomises aspects of George MacDonald's thought which were to be prominent in his later life and work. There was the Gordon element, which typifies his Celtic background, his romantic imagination, his sense of high drama and his mystic vision. The second element is Death itself. Mortality was never very far from MacDonald. He saw friends and family die before their time, and he himself was close to death from illness many times in his life. The idea of Death was something he had to come to terms with from an early age. It was never an easy task, but as he grew up he learned to use his Celtic imagination together with his growing Christian faith to develop a concept of Death as an ultimate good, not as something to be dreaded and feared.

Thoughts of Death as a personal threat (or blessing) were far in the future for the little boy thoughtfully watching the funeral procession. He may have watched from the window of his home, a house built by his father in the town's main thoroughfare, Duke Street.

The presence of the MacDonald family in Gordon country was, according to their own tradition, due to the Glencoe Massacre of 1692, when a regiment of Campbell soldiers slaughtered those members of the MacDonald clan who lived in Glencoe. Alastir MacDonald, half-brother of the old chief Alexander MacIain MacDonald, escaped with his family and

2

headed for Gordon country, knowing that the Duke of Gordon would receive him sympathetically. Alastir's son settled at Portsoy, on the coast north of Huntly, and became a quarry-man, dealing in the marble to be found at Portsoy. He had his own land nearby, which he farmed. His son, William, was George MacDonald's great-grandfather. Like his grandfather he was involved in the tragic events of his own day. He joined the forces of Bonnie Prince Charlie as a piper—a place of high rank—and was present at the slaughter at Culloden. He fled back to Portsoy and hid for a time in the caves which abound in the cliffs overlooking the sea. William went blind and his land was confiscated, but no further penalty was exacted for this part in the insurrection, and eventually he was able to resume his post as Town Piper of Portsoy.

His youngest son, named Charles Edward after the Preten-der, came to Huntly to find work. In the latter half of the eight-eenth century Huntly had a thriving linen industry depending on cottage labour. Many of the neat thatched houses had sunken floors to accommodate weaving looms. There was a large bleach-works, for whitening the finished cloth, and here Charles Edward MacDonald found employment as a clerk. He prospered, and was taken into partnership with the owners, the MacVeagh brothers. When they died he was left the sole owner. He took over the works and expanded the business, building a factory which made thread, mainly for export to South America.

In 1778 Charles married a Huntly girl, Isabella Robertson. She was a zealous Protestant of strong character; although we cannot know for certain, we may surmise that owing to her influence Charles MacDonald abandoned the Roman Cath-olic faith of his father and his ancestors. Certainly his children were brought up as staunch Presbyterians, though the family later transferred to the Congregational Church.

Isabella MacDonald exerted a large influence on all her family, not least upon her grandson George. Her faith was, as with so many Scots in the Calvinist tradition, deep and strong, but also severe and gloomy. Her main efforts were in a nega-tive direction—she wished to avoid sin at all costs. Drinking whisky or profaning the Sabbath with music and singing were things she would not tolerate. When she found out that her third son Charles had a violin she burned it.

She was an active and vigorous woman, with a good head for business. She helped her husband to run the bank he opened in his home, acting as agent for an Aberdeen bank. For this she needed a safe, so she emptied the family papers out of the 'chanter kist' (a chest in which bagpipes and other objects of value were deposited) and used that. The MacDonald family had kept its own records of births, marriages and deaths, for as Roman Catholics they were not included in the Parish Register. Isabella burned them, thus causing great trouble and annoyance to her descendants, who could no longer prove their descent beyond her father-in-law. Her Protestant zeal was glad to see these 'snares of the Devil' go up in flames. She was also canny enough to realise that even these indications of a family's former adherence to Roman Catholicism might possibly prove dangerous in a period when religious differences were strongly felt.

Besides her own nine children Isabella adopted four beggar children and set them on their way in the world. At least one of these ended his days prosperously. Nor did her good works end here. She subscribed to the London City Mission and was the inspiration of the Huntly temperance movement. Her eldest son William built a brewery in Huntly and prospered. We do not know her reaction to this: did she sever all connection with him? Or did beer escape her recriminations as not being under the temperance ban? She seems, at any rate, to have had closer relationships with her next three sons, George, Charles and James. When Charles Edward died, these three inherited the bleach-works, and Charles received in addition the bank-agency. He was possibly the favourite son in spite of his back-sliding with the violin.

Business was good, and in 1821 the three brothers sought to extend the bleach-works. They leased a farm, known simply as 'The Farm', from the fourth Duke of Gordon. It was situated at Upper Pirriesmill, on the east bank of the River Bogie, about half a mile from Huntly, and had meadows sloping down to the river which were ideal for laying out the bleached linen to dry. Lactic acid was used for the bleaching, this being obtained from The Farm's cows, and a water-wheel on the Bogie provided power for the operation.

The Farm had no accommodation suitable for the MacDonald family, and George, the second son, had two houses built in Duke Street. They were contiguous, with a connecting door between. Isabella MacDonald lived in one, her son in the other. In 1822 George brought his bride home to this house. She was Helen MacKay, daughter of a Captain MacKay from Sutherland, and was beautiful, gifted and intelligent. She was readily accepted in the family and the neighbourhood, some even going so far as to believe that Mr and Mrs MacDonald were the best-looking couple in the whole parish. While living in Duke Street they had two children: Charles, born in 1823, and George—our hero—on 10 December 1824.

George and his younger brother James decided to move out to The Farm, although it meant going to the trouble of building a house there. One is tempted to wonder whether the close proximity of old Mrs MacDonald was a factor in the decision. She was certainly loved and respected by her sons and by her daughter-in-law; nevertheless, her strength of character may have been overpowering at close quarters. There was also the consideration that Helen MacDonald was unwell, and would benefit from country air and fresh farm food. She suffered from tuberculosis, and found herself unable to feed her baby son George for more than the first few weeks. He had to be fed by a wet-nurse, and 'cryed desperate a while the first night'[2] at this change in his regime, as his mother reported in a letter to her mother-in-law (who was visiting in Aberdeen at the time).

In 1826 the new house was completed and the two families of George and James MacDonald settled in. It was called 'Bleachfield Cottage' at first, but this was dropped after a while, and the whole settlement, house and farm-buildings a furlong away, was known collectively as 'The Farm'. It was not a large house by nineteenth-century standards, especially considering that it was occupied by two families, each with children. James had a daughter, Margaret, and a son, James. Four more boys were born there to George and Helen MacDonald. James was born there soon after the move (how did they distinguish him from his cousin James?), then came Alexander, and John MacKay who died as a baby. Another boy was born a year or so later. He was also named John, with Hill as his second name, possibly after the Minister of the Congregational Church, who was a close friend of his parents.

This brought the total number living at The Farm, not counting servants, to eleven. The problem of space was alleviated by the installation of box beds in some of the living rooms, but undoubtedly the crowded conditions encouraged the spread of tuberculosis. Helen was not the only sufferer. In 1825 her husband had had to have a leg amputated because of a tuberculous infection of the knee. In the days before the discovery of chloroform he bore the operation with characteristic fortitude, refusing the customary stiff glass of whisky.

The completion of George MacDonald's family brings us to 1831 or 1832, by which time they had begun to run into difficulties. Charles, being over-optimistic in his speculations with the bank-agency, had got heavily into debt. He absconded to America, leaving his two brothers George and James to take on his liabilities. Whether they were legally responsible is uncertain, but as they were his partners in the bleach-works they felt responsible for the bank-agency too. They spent the rest of their lives paying off the debts that Charles had incurred.

Then in 1832, not long after the birth of John Hill, Helen MacDonald died of tuberculosis. Young George was only eight years old, and he recovered quickly from his loss, the more so as he had seen little of his mother during her last illness. He had a lasting impression of her sweet face as she bent over him, and a poignant memory of her with John MacKay. In later life he included this along with other childhood recollections in his semi-autobiographical book, *Ranald Bannerman's Boyhood*. The four- or five-year-old George remembered

> looking out of my bed one night and seeing my mother bending over [the baby] in her lap ... I fell asleep, but by and by woke and looked out again. No-one was there. Not only were mother and baby gone, but the cradle was gone too. I knew that my little brother was dead. I did not cry: I was too young and ignorant to cry about it.[3]

Apart from this, George's memories of his childhood centred

largely on his father, and on the games he had with his brothers. The boys were looked after for a while by their aunt, Christina MacKay, and her love helped to fill the gap left by their mother.

*

There were two schools in Huntly at this time, the Parish Church school, and the 'Adventure School' in Stewart Lane, run by the Rev. Colin Stewart. The MacDonalds did not by this time attend the Parish Church (which was Presbyterian); although her husband had been an elder there, Isabella Mac-Donald thought its minister's preaching and teaching ineffectual, so she betook herself and her family to the Congregational or Missionar Church (as it was known at that time in Scotland) that had just been established in the town. It may have been this that caused George MacDonald senior to send his boys to the Adventure School rather than to the Parish School. There was little difference between the schools, both being run by licentiates of the Church of Scotland, and both charging a small fee for attendance. It was possible for even poor people to send their children to school, as assistance was available from the parish towards school expenses, and parish-assisted pupils attended either school. In fact, the Adventure School probably only came into being because the Parish School was too small to take all the children in the parish. However, the boys at the two schools considered themselves rivals, and occasionally there would be battles between the two groups, with stones flying so furiously that it was a wonder to the adult George, looking back, that so little damage was done. He had a weak chest, with a tendency to bronchitis and asthma, which made him a poor stone-thrower, so he acted a general's part, collecting piles of stones and marshalling his friends for furious charges down the hill to the rival school.

Scottish children had to attend school on Saturday mornings for the learning of the Shorter Catechism, that bastion of the Presbyterian faith. It was formulated by the Puritan divines of Westminster in 1647, and by 1830 its quaint prose

7

would have been largely unintelligible to most children. Learning by heart was required, but not understanding; there was little attempt at explanation, and learning was thereby rendered more difficult. Young George felt this keenly, not so much for himself, for he was a good learner, and moreover could always ask his father to explain the Catechism to him, but for the other less fortunate children on whom the teacher's wrath fell very heavily.

MacDonald had ample cause to remember Colin Stewart, and he portrayed him in his novel, *Alec Forbes of Howglen*, as Murdoch Malison the schoolmaster, or 'dominie', who has a vicious sense of justice, and severely punishes the slightest mistake on the part of any child. The MacDonald boys believed that Stewart's thrashings were partly responsible for the death of their brother James at the age of eight. Later Stewart emigrated to Australia. The total effect of his teaching on George had been to give him a hearty dislike of school in general and learning by rote in particular, and to implant in him a lifelong aversion to the Shorter Catechism. The Catechism begins with this sentiment: 'The chief end of man is to glorify God and to enjoy him for ever.' In *Alec Forbes of Howglen* MacDonald was to write, 'For my part, I wish the spiritual engineers who constructed it had, after laying the grandest foundation-stone that truth could afford them, glorified God by going no further.'

Young George was often glad to miss school, even at the price of frequent attacks of bronchitis and asthma, particularly in the winter and spring months. He probably lost little as far as his education goes, for he was an avid reader, and during his illnesses would have had ample time to sample the family's library, such as it was. There would certainly have been a copy of the Bible in the Authorised Version, and probably an edition of Shakespeare's Plays. MacDonald's work shows an intimate knowledge of both. There was also *The Pilgrim's Progress*, Milton's *Paradise Lost* and Klopstock's *Messiah*; this last was an English translation of a German poem dealing with the death and resurrection of Christ, and written in imitation of Milton.

George would probably also have sampled the *Night*

Thoughts of Edward Young, a contemporary of Alexander Pope. This long work, although prevailingly gloomy, yet contains several ideas about the spiritual world which were to be a feature of MacDonald's mature philosophy. As for children's books, MacDonald has this to say in *Ranald Bannerman's Boyhood*:

> I had got the loan of Mrs. Trimmer's story of the family of robins [*The Robins*, first published in 1786] and was every now and then reading a page of it with unspeakable delight. We had very few books for children in those days and in that far out-of-the-way place, and those we did get were the more dearly prized.[5]

In spite of his mother's death, his illness and his fierce schoolmaster, MacDonald's boyhood was essentially a happy one. His father provided an environment of sincere affection and consistent discipline. It was not in those days considered right to show one's affection towards one's children, but the MacDonald boys were nonetheless aware of their father's love. When in need of comfort the young George always turned to his father. George MacDonald senior did not put too many restrictions on his boys—in fact he was inclined to laugh if anyone complained to him of their wildness—but he did insist on their doing as they were told, and his 'rebuke was awful indeed, if he found even the youngest guilty of untruth, or cruelty, or injustice.'[6]

He had a fine sense of humour. Here is a typical example related by Greville MacDonald:

> He would declare, and in such a way that no little hearers could disbelieve him, that twice every day the Aberdeen coach *Defiance* and its four horses drove between his legs. My sisters and I had it only from our Uncle Charles, and no questioning could extort any sort of explanation. But at last our mother took pity upon our fear that the obdurate uncle might be deceiving us. The explanation was this, that though our grandfather had his right leg always with him, the other was buried in the graveyard far away on the other side of the high road.[7]

In later life George MacDonald the writer often caused friends and relations to shake their heads with disapproval over his reckless generosity. In this, however, he was following

9

his father's example. When a young visitor to The Farm remarked that he found it difficult in Aberdeen without a watch, Mr MacDonald took out his own silver turnip watch and handed it over, saying that the sun was a better time-keeper in Strathbogie than any watch in Aberdeen. And he never afterwards wore a replacement.

Although he did not spend much time with his boys when they were small, he set aside summer Sunday afternoons and winter weekday evenings to be with them. MacDonald remembers that

> he would sit for an hour talking away to us in his gentle, slow, deep voice, telling us story after story out of ... [the Bible], sometimes reading a few verses, sometimes turning the bare facts into an expanded and illustrated narrative of his own ... I shall never forget Joseph in Egypt hearing the pattering of the asses' hoofs in the street, and throwing up the window, and looking out, and seeing all his own brothers coming riding towards him.[8]

MacDonald senior was tall and, in his later years, had receding white hair and long sidewhiskers meeting in a small beard. He usually wore a blue swallow-tail coat with gilt buttons, black and white check trousers, and a cravat tied loosely under a soft collar.

His son's relationship with him was to grow into a deep and abiding friendship as George grew up and left home. In the many letters he wrote home he shared with his father his hopes and fears, his aspirations and depressions. He portrayed him in his first novel as David Elginbrod, the wise old Scot whose influence pervades the whole book. But the greatest thing his father did for him, he considered, was by the excellence of his fatherhood to give him an insight into the fatherhood of God. He dedicated his second volume of poems to him, writing,

> Thou hast been faithful to my highest need;
> And I, thy debtor, ever, evermore,
> Shall never feel the grateful burden sore.
> Yet most I thank thee, not for any deed,
> But for the sense thy living self did breed,
> Of fatherhood still at the great world's core.[9]

The MacDonald boys all enjoyed a wonderful freedom to go where they liked when they liked. It originated in their mother's last illness, when they were encouraged, for the sake of keeping the house quiet, to be out all day and every day. There was plenty for them to do, even when they were not at school. The farm was a constant source of interest, with all its activities from ploughing to threshing for them to watch or perhaps lend a hand with. The boys learned to ride on the farm horses, at first going on their backs when they were led out to water, then taking them to the field to graze—a more risky business as they were liable to fling up their heads and gallop away. MacDonald learned to love horses, and developed a wonderful ability to communicate with them in such a way that they would always respond to his encouragement. A tired horse would always step out with fresh vigour if MacDonald took the reins. His father had a mare called Missy of whom George was particularly fond. He used to stand by her in the meadow, flicking away the flies, or lie on her back reading his book as she patiently grazed. When she died at a great age he kept one of her hoofs as a paperweight.

If he tired of the horses he could always seek the company of the cattle and the cowherd, a lad of great ingenuity in devising games and toys. Or there was the River Bogie which, with its weir and mill-race, provided deep pools for swimming and boating. It could also provide excitement in the shape of floods: the water-level could rise very quickly, particularly in the autumn with its heavy rains. In 1829 the Bogie and the Deveron both overflowed, causing widespread flooding. Mac-Donald included an account of this in *Alec Forbes of Howglen*, and no doubt in the description of a flood in *Sir Gibbie* he was also drawing on his memories of the rivers in flood. He described how haystacks and bedsteads came bobbing down the valley, and how afterwards salmon and rabbits were to be found entangled in the branches of trees. There was good fishing to be had in quieter times when the water was at its usual level—the local lads used to pull hair from the horses' tails for their fishing lines, at the risk of a sharp kick!

Huntly itself provided entertainment, with its weekly market day, when shepherds and drovers would gather from the country for miles around. On such days young George would hurry from school—it closed at three o'clock—to the Gordon Arms, where many of them would be enjoying their whisky and telling over their local news. MacDonald listened assiduously, and picked up many details of crofter life which he was to use later in his books. These shepherds spoke in Gaelic. MacDonald knew enough to follow the drift of a story, but he never learned to speak it himself, to his lasting regret.

Storytelling was a good way of passing the long, cold winter evenings, and MacDonald had many friends in the town or on the farm who excelled in this. In a community where many were illiterate, the art of the sennachie or storyteller was rated highly; and it was no doubt from such people that MacDonald himself learned to tell a story in masterly fashion. He also spent some of those long evenings making things; he was deft with his hands even into old age. In *Gutta Percha Willie* he describes how Willie makes a toy water wheel, and this must be something that he had attempted to make for himself. Willie has a try at all sorts of crafts—knitting, spinning, cobbling and shoeing a horse; in a community such as Huntly there would be plenty of people who would be willing to show an inquiring youngster how to use the tools of their particular trade.

Another pastime for indoors was playing at church-going, and on more than one occasion the young George MacDonald would jump up on a table and take to task the maid or his brothers in mock-solemn tones. Much later, when he was studying for the ministry, his father reminded him of his boyhood 'preaching sessions':

> when I think of it, [your brothers] have repeatedly heard you long ago, when the basin-stand was your pulpit, and when matters *purely local* and *domestic* formed the leading subjects of your prayers before your congregation. I believe you have to thank your own *slim form* that you were not overtaken by the same awkward kind of calamity which befel *one of the brotherhood*, who, having got by force and the impulse of his own greater gravitation into the aforesaid *pulpit*, found when he had occasion to slip out again, that to do so was no easy matter; nay, it was an impossibility until he had discharged his audience, and, having more privately peeled off his trousers, made a shift to crawl out of his involuntary imprison-

ment! Take care, man, and don't ever preach in too small a pulpit for fear of the consequences![10]

There were summer holidays, too—trips to the seaside at Portsoy or at Banff, both on the coast to the north of Huntly. Banff was the home of MacDonald's uncle George Mackay, who had two daughters. One of them, Helen, was to play an important part in MacDonald's studenthood and courtship. The very first letter written by George MacDonald to his father was sent from Portsoy, when young George was nine years old. He mentions that he has been in the sea, and that his aunt [Christina?] makes him drink the water, which he doesn't like so much! This was, of course, a period when sea-water, taken both internally and externally, was thought to be beneficial for all kinds of ills.

Better times came to the Adventure School when, on Mr Stewart's departure in 1835, his place was taken by the Rev Alexander Millar. This new teacher noticed how quick young George was at learning his tasks, and began to take an interest in him. He introduced him to the classics of English literature and encouraged him to write poetry of his own. He wrote a poem on 'Patriotism' for an examination, and was invited to read it aloud by one of the examining ministers. In his early teens Millar set him to teach some of the younger children in the school—a common arrangement in those days—and before long George began to help with the evening classes which Millar gave for working men and women. He sometimes accompanied Millar to his home after school, where Millar would read passages from his favourite books to the young lad. MacDonald needed nothing more to open his eyes and ears to the beauties of literature; he commented in *Ranald Bannerman's Boyhood* that to hear another person read aloud is to become aware of all sorts of nuances of meaning and beauty that one has missed in one's own reading. He learned too from Millar a secret of expounding literature that was to make him a teacher of outstanding worth: it is simply to gain the respect of your pupils and show them what you value:

If a man in whom you have confidence merely lays his finger on a paragraph and says to you, 'Read that,' you will probably discover three times as much in it as you would if you had only chanced upon it in the course of your reading.[11]

When MacDonald was nearly thirteen he and three other boys formed the Huntly Juvenile Temperance Society. His grandmother was a moving force behind the Huntly temperance movement, and she mentioned the formation of the Society in her diary. Much harm was done to many people by easy access to cheap liquor, particularly whisky. The Huntly Juvenile Temperance Society declared: 'We agree to abstain from distilled spirits except for medicinal purposes and to discountenance the causes and practice of Intemperance'[12]—a very moderate declaration compared with those of the more extreme teetotal movements that were to spring up in England. A juvenile temperance society was necessary because there were no laws prohibiting the sale of alcohol to juniors; indeed, small babies were often fed with gin by their poverty-stricken parents—it was cheaper than milk. The meetings were held in the MacDonald thread factory, with young George in the chair. One of its members reported that he always 'spoke like a book'.

The MacDonald family, as might be expected of the sons and grandsons of Isabella MacDonald, was deeply religious. George MacDonald senior was a deacon of the Congregational Church and a close friend of its minister, John Hill. Every Monday morning he would call on Mr Hill and they would talk and pray together. No doubt the MacDonald boys went to church every Sunday with their father, but George seems to have had few happy memories associated with church-going. In *Alec Forbes of Howglen* the main impressions which the young Annie Anderson receives from the Congregational Church are of lengthy sermons which arouse in her a fear that she is doomed to hell-fire for eternity. However good a man Mr Hill may have been, he could not counter the gloomy and oppressive spiritual atmosphere fostered by Scottish Calvinism. Meeting it as he did in church and school, the young MacDonald was on the whole repelled by it, and he was to do much heart-searching before he was able to reject the bad and accept the good in his national religion.

In 1839, when George was fourteen, his father married again. His second wife was Margaret McColl, who had been a close friend of Helen MacDonald. Greville MacDonald has this to say of her:

> The new wife took the place of the mother in the hearts of both father and boys; indeed my father owed to her everything that the most devoted of mothers can give. My own intimacy with her—for she died only in 1910 in her 102nd year, all her faculties except hearing unimpaired—revealed a tenderness of heart, a patience in adversity, a penetrating wisdom, together with a power of sympathy that account for much of the Celt's characteristic charm. She was pure Highland. The boys' new mother found her task less onerous than usually befalls. She used to say that one of the first things that struck her in her new home was the fine manners and courtesy of all the boys. If one of the elders rose to leave the room, either George or Alec would be always beforehand to open the door. She could not drop a thimble or a ball of wool, but it was instantly picked up for her.[13]

She gave the boys three new sisters, Isabella, Louisa and Jane, but as they were born after George had left home he did not see a great deal of them when they were small.

The MacDonald business enterprise had meanwhile run into trouble. Spinning mills in big towns such as Glasgow made the thread-factory unprofitable and it had to close. New and more efficient methods of bleaching were discovered and the old methods abandoned. The MacDonalds recovered by putting the water wheel to a new use—manufacturing potato flour and starch. Even the potato-rind was not wasted, but was processed to make a dressing for coarse canvas bags. The starch was advertised as '*Farina*, a substitute for arrowroot and suitable for invalids and children's diet'. However, the three successive years of potato-blight in 1846–8, which brought hardship to the Highlands of Scotland as well as to Ireland, put an end to this business. After this the brothers put the wheel to a more common use in grinding oats, so that from being the son of a prosperous industrialist, George MacDonald senior became a miller. He was not one to worry about loss of standing, however, and as long as he could afford to feed and clothe his boys, and to pay for their education, he was con-

15

tent. The boys always had plenty of good, plain food, and they were adequately clothed, if somewhat shabby.

It was during the famine caused by the potato-blight that MacDonald senior by his compassion and good-humour averted a riot in Huntly. A rumour had spread that the MacDonald brothers were keeping back their grain until the price had risen even higher than it was already, and a mob set off from the town in an ugly mood, intending to burn an effigy of MacDonald senior in front of his cottage. Jane, his youngest daughter, had just been born, and it had been a difficult delivery; Margaret was out of danger, but needed rest and quiet. Greville MacDonald continues the tale:

> My grandfather had just taken off his artificial leg and set it beside the fire, as was his wont when tired. He quickly replaced it and hurried down to stop their entry into the garden.
>
> They were so much taken aback that their anger was immediately silenced. He told them that absolute quiet was essential if his wife was to win through, and he begged them to go down to the market and tell him there what the trouble was all about. Without one word of protest, they departed somewhat shamefacedly, carrying the effigy with them.
>
> By the time my grandfather reached them in the market-place, however, they were joined by others and their anger revived. They built a bonfire ... with the clumsy effigy sprawling on top, its wooden leg ridiculously in evidence. When at last they were ready to kindle the faggots and my grandfather appeared ... the crowd burst into indignant rage. Quite unperturbed, however, he began to address them, when their hootings were instantly stilled. 'Bide a wee, lads,' he shouted, 'afore ye set the corp alow (aflame). *Ye've fastened the timmer-leg to the wrang hurdie* (hip).' And leaning on his stick he gravely added: 'Noo, ye's gang on wi' yer ploys wi' a guid conscience, an' burn yer auld freen'!'
>
> Thus were the hungry set laughing and presently cheering the man their hearts knew if their minds misjudged. Then, at his invitation, a few went with him back to The Farm to be convinced that its barn, like their own meal-tubs, was empty.[14]

2

The student 1840–50

Scotland was famous in the early nineteenth century for its scholars as well as for its poverty. The education system was geared to the poor scholar. As we have seen, help could be obtained to pay the few shillings' fees of the parish schools; university fees were also low, and there were bursaries to help those of high ability and low income. Moreover, the sessions ran from November to March, so that students could earn enough by working in the summer to keep themselves during their winter studies. Students could not 'live in' as they did at Oxford and Cambridge; they had to find cheap lodgings in the university towns, sharing accommodation, and sometimes a bed, to reduce costs.

With Mr Millar's encouragement it was decided that George should go to the university at Aberdeen, and as he needed to enter for the Bursary Competition he was sent when he was fifteen for preliminary coaching in Latin at the Aulton Grammar School in Aberdeen. He stayed there for three months, from August to October, and drew on this experience when he came to write *Robert Falconer*. In this novel he says of the school,

> If the school work was dry it was thorough. If that academy had no sweetly shadowing trees ... beyond still was the sea and the sky; and [the] court, morning and afternoon, was filled with the shouts of eager boys, kicking the football with mad rushings to and fro, and sometimes with woundings and faintings.[1]

He sat for a bursary in November and came twelfth, winning the Fullarton Bursary of £14 per annum, which was enough to pay his fees and some of his expenses during the five months' session. He entered King's College, Aberdeen, in November 1840.

Students worked for a Master's degree, and the course comprised four annual sessions, the first two concentrating on the standard academic subjects of Greek, Latin and mathematics. A majority of students, intending to be ministers, would thereafter specialise in moral philosophy and theological subjects. Courses were also available in the sciences, both experimental and mathematical. MacDonald chose to read chemistry and natural philosophy—what we might call physical science. The University authorities did not prescribe fixed courses of study for the students; rather, the students were free to attend any classes whether or not they intended to follow them to degree level. So it came about that MacDonald would have been able to attend anatomy classes at the Medical School as well as his regular classes.

While it is not certain that he did attend these it is highly likely in view of the details he gives of the anatomical classes Alec attends in *Alec Forbes of Howglen*. The Resurrectionist scandal which exposed the murders committed by Burke and Hare in Edinburgh and Williams and Bishop in London, in order to supply corpses for anatomy classes, had occurred a little before his time, around 1830. However, public antagonism to anatomy doubtless lingered on into the 1840s, and MacDonald uses this background for a lively scene in which the Aberdeen mob chases Alec over the roof-tops to his lodgings.

George MacDonald did not complete his course until five years had elapsed, for he had to miss the session of 1842–3. This was owing to financial difficulties at home; the lowering of grain prices meant that many small farmers were suffering financially, and the MacDonald brothers were no exception. George's father was unable to send the oatmeal and potatoes on which George lived while at Aberdeen, and so for that year he left the University and sought employment.

It is clear from the many references in his books that he spent a period at this formative time in his life cataloguing and arranging a neglected library in a stately home. It is most likely that this occurred during the inter-sessionary year; Greville MacDonald suggests the summer of 1842. It was probably at Thurso Castle that he was employed so congenially, although the library there is no longer in existence. Mr Millar had introduced him to the classics of English literature, but here he found a great treasury of books with which he was as yet unacquainted. He sampled the sixteenth century poets, and found a source of great delight in the medieval romances. He had already begun to read German, and now found many of the German classics, of which he wrote in *The Portent*, 'I found in these volumes a mine of wealth inexhaustible'.[2] In his novels he refers particularly to Jean-Paul [Richter], to Goethe, to Schiller and to Heinrich Heine, as well as to Novalis. Mac-Donald also knew Carlyle's translations of the German romances as well as his life of Jean-Paul and his translations of Jean-Paul's 'dream-passages', although he was perhaps more likely to have obtained these in Aberdeen than Thurso. The library played an important part in the development of his imagination, showing him what treasures lay beyond the bounds of academic scholarship (English Literature was not a university subject in Scotland).

We do not know how MacDonald spent the latter part of 1842; he may have returned to Huntly, contributing his earnings to the upkeep of his family in these lean years. If so, he would have enjoyed making friends with his eighteen-months-old sister Isabella. In February 1843 he returned to Aberdeen and obtained a post teaching arithmetic at Aberdeen Central Academy; its headmaster reported that he taught 'with great spirit and skill'. He kept the post until November, when he was able once more to resume his studies at the University. He obtained his degree in April 1845, taking the third prize in chemistry and the fourth prize in natural philosophy.

While the standards of the Scottish universities were not especially high compared with those in England, the grounding they gave in the basic subjects was thorough, and they did foster independence of thought. It was while he was a student that MacDonald began to think for himself and, after much heart-searching, to develop the particular approach to the material and spiritual worlds which was to characterise his writing. He was not alone, but often felt himself to be lonely; the deep thought which he gave to philosophical issues probably set him at a distance from his fellow students. He was rapidly acquiring a reputation as an individualist, particularly in his dress; he wore a bright tartan coat with a regulation scarlet gown of minimal size draped, or flying out, behind him. He was a member of the Debating Society, and also often took part in charades—then a fashionable amusement—at the houses of his friends, being noted for his ingenuity in devising crazy costumes. On one occasion he wanted buttons for an old green coat, so cut a large carrot into discs and sewed them on—to the huge delight of all present.

But he was often moody and depressed. His friend Robert Troup, who was later to marry his cousin Margaret, said of him,

> I have recollections of him sitting by himself ... silent and thoughtful, sometimes apparently musing, and sometimes reading while the others were talking. At other times he took his part heartily in the conversation that was going on ... His older friends were anxious about his spiritual state.[3]

He would sometimes leave his circle of friends in the town and wander on the links or the sea-shore. He always loved the sea, and at this particular period he felt he shared in its turmoil and its peace, in its rejection of man's authority. Occasionally he would walk with another friend, James Maconochie. Once they went out in the evening to watch a storm:

> When Maconochie returned about midnight ... he looked anxious and disturbed, and said: 'I hope George MacDonald is not going out of his mind ... When we got to the shore, he walked backwards and forwards on the sands amid the howling winds and the beating spray, with the waves coming up to our feet; and all the time he went on addressing the sea and the waves and the storm.'[4]

Would MacDonald have behaved so erratically if Maconochie had not been there to see him? He seems to have had a streak of exhibitionism in his character, as evidenced mainly by his oddities of dress. There can be no doubt that he felt very deeply the anguish, confusion and torment of soul that he was giving vent to. But he must have found satisfaction in having an audience to hear and witness his outburst. He needed to communicate, to express himself to others. It was this very trait of his personality that was to make him, first an author, and secondly a lecturer and actor.

Maconochie had no need to fear for his friend's sanity, for MacDonald continued to take part in many constructive activities. He assisted at the Blackfriars Congregational Church, teaching in the Sunday School and no doubt helping the minister, Dr John Kennedy, in his attempts to provide education and food for the countless beggar-children who roamed the streets of Aberdeen. But he was becoming more and more ill at ease with the basic Calvinist doctrines, which he perceived as portraying God as a jealous, vindictive being who takes a delight in punishing people. The doctrine of predestination was a particular stumbling-block to him, for it made it seem as if God deliberately created some people that they might be doomed to eternal torment, and others that they might receive his special favour. He remembered his grandmother's agony over the fate she believed was in store for his Uncle Charles, and felt that he did not want a God whose love was partial and therefore unjust.

Other Christians were thinking along similar lines. While MacDonald was a student there was raging throughout the Congregational Church in Scotland a controversy over the doctrine of universal redemption, which the Calvinists denied. Some students were expelled from the Glasgow Theological College for saying that Christ's redemption was available to all, not just 'the elect'. MacDonald found himself involved in this debate, much to the concern of Dr Kennedy of Blackfriars, himself a stern Calvinist. It began to dawn on MacDonald that religion is not adherence to a set of doctrines such as those expressed in the Westminster Confession or the Shorter Catechism. He knew that he needed a God in whom he could believe wholeheartedly, a God who would be all in all.

His spiritual quest generated a chaos of thoughts and feelings, and he expressed some of these in poetry. The idea of a mystical quest was one of his themes; he also wrote about the Harrowing of Hell, exploring the concept that death is a blessing, not a curse. He made many translations from the German poets. He corresponded with his cousin Helen from Banff, now at school in London, in whose sympathy he found great comfort. She was nearly three years older than himself, beautiful and highly educated, with a lovely voice; she was also an excellent pianist. MacDonald fancied himself in love with her, and wrote her a whole series of love poems. He idealised himself as a poet-lover, and elevated Helen as the Ideal Woman—a romantic dream which could not stand the test of reality. He later grew easily out of his infatuation and kept up a happy relationship with her for the rest of his life, including in his letters humorous passages in broad Aberdeenshire dialect.

As well as the intimate verses which were for her eyes alone, he wrote out for her an album of poems including some of his own verse, together with 'The Rime of the Ancient Mariner', parts of Shelley's 'The Wandering Jew' and extracts from such poets as Mrs Hemans and James Hogg. The following verse, taken from the book, illustrates the dominant mood of MacDonald's writing at this period:

> Bury me, bury me deep
> In some lonely cove on the wild sea's shore.
> There none o'er my grave will come and weep:
> But the maddened waves' tempest-roar
> Will soothe this spirit when, shrouded in gloom,
> It visits its rough and unlettered tomb![5]

He also included in the book a blank verse narrative entitled 'David' intended as a companion-piece to Browning's 'Saul'. He submitted this, after some polishing, for publication in the *Congregational Magazine*. It appeared in February 1846, his first work in print. He also attempted a poetic drama in two acts, called 'Gennaro' and inspired by Byron's 'Manfred', but he never completed it.

However, poetry could not earn him a living, and he had to find a more practical way of keeping himself. He was interested in medicine and would have liked to become a doctor, but his father had not the money to provide the extra equipment and training he would need. He also considered chemistry as a profession, and wished to go to Germany to study with von Liebig, the chemist who had been one of the discoverers of chloroform, but was again prevented by lack of

22

money. In the eyes of his friends and advisers the Congregational ministry was an obvious choice of career, but MacDonald would not enter the Church merely to gain himself a living. In any case, he had doubts as to his suitability. He felt he was not the right sort of person to be a pastor, and he was not ready to take on responsibility for other souls than his own. Finally, rather as a stop-gap than as a definite choice, and with the knowledge that he was a good teacher, he moved to London to seek a post as a tutor.

Dr John Morison was an old friend of George MacDonald senior, and had taken the liberal side, opposing Dr Kennedy, in the universal redemption controversy. He was now one of the most fashionable preachers in London, and was to be heard at the Trevor Chapel, Brompton. He found a post for young George with one of the members of his congregation who lived at Fulham. MacDonald taught his three little boys for about two years, and found his work highly uncongenial. The boys were priggish and ignorant, one asking if Jesus Christ was crucified four times—although his elder brother indignantly insisted that it was only twice! There were two sisters as well, whose unruly screaming made life difficult for MacDonald; he was not employed to teach them, but it seems they were allowed to disturb their brothers' studies.

MacDonald drew on his memories of the family when he portrayed the Appleditches in his novel *David Elginbrod*; the parents are well-to-do tradespeople, inordinately proud of their dull sons, whom they intend to train as ministers. Hugh Sutherland, the young tutor, has problems disciplining the boys, who are rude and cheeky, because of the mother's interference. Sutherland maintains some independence because he has his own lodgings, but MacDonald lived with the family in Fulham, which gave him extra problems. His employers were not intentionally unkind to him, but they did not give him the care which his weak health demanded. They may have been misled by his fine physique into supposing that he was as strong as he looked. The boys' mother, in fact, resented him, and the effort needed to conciliate her drained his spirits and often made him depressed. He was expected to take his charges twice every Sunday to the Trevor Chapel, which he

found irksome; he wanted to devote some of the time to wor-
shipping on his own. He still had spiritual difficulties, which
he discussed with Dr Morison. He also wrote about them to his
father. He was not by now so much troubled about the im-
placability of Calvinism as by the question of whether his own
faith was sufficient and lasting. He had seen the loveliness of
Christ, and was attempting to follow him, but the attempt revealed so much that was lacking in himself that he doubted
whether he could call himself a Christian at all. But by November 1845 he must have been coming to some understanding of
his difficulty, for he wrote to his father, 'My error seems to be
always searching for faith in place of contemplating the truths
of the gospel which produce faith. My spirit is often very con-
fused.'[6] He had less time now for reading than he had had as a
student, but he did manage to improve his mind 'steadily,
though it may be slowly',[7] as he put it in the same letter to his
father. He recommended to him Darwin's account of the
voyage of the *Beagle*, which he was reading with some enjoy-
ment.

The tedium of life in Fulham was relieved by meetings with
his cousin Helen, now married to Alexander Powell, son of a
prosperous leather merchant. MacDonald was introduced to
the Powell family at their home in Upper Clapton, an old
Georgian house called 'The Limes'. James Powell, Helen's
father-in-law, was a deeply religious man, a Nonconformist.
His wife was an invalid, and his eldest daughter Charlotte, a
very strong-minded young woman, had charge of the family,
which comprised two boys and six girls. Although they had a
great love for one another, the upbringing of the children had
been severe, in accordance with Nonconformist principles.
Such entertainments as the theatre, cards and dancing were
forbidden, and music was limited to religious and classical per-
formances. The family was in fact very musical: they used to
astonish visitors by singing grace before meals in exquisite harmony, and old Mr Powell himself was a very fine violin player.
They were also very good actors; since they felt that play-
acting was wrong, they confined themselves to drawing-room
charades.

The girls had been taught music, reading, writing and arithmetic at home, but after this their education had been limited, consisting chiefly in religious devotions. Correctness in doctrinal matters and religious observance was very important to them, and the introduction to their circle of the bright and bewitching Helen MacKay was something of a shock. She conveyed the impression that her outlook was wider than they had ever dared to contemplate, yet at the same time she was entirely orthodox and devout in her observances. The four youngest girls, Louisa, Angela, Florentia and Caroline, were quickly charmed by her, and were eager to meet her cousin George, whose introduction to the family soon brought about a complete change of atmosphere. He charmed Angela, then aged about nineteen, by treating her as an equal, whereas her family considered her something of a fool for her inability to spell and memorise. Even in their teens the girls were sometimes treated like little children, but George's ready sympathy enabled them to bear their treatment with some equanimity. Angela remembered that

> Once when I was ill he came to see me in the old schoolroom, because I was naughty and would not take my castor oil. He had not talked to me for many minutes before I gulped it down without a murmur, and was rewarded next day with a box of sugar-candy—a rare luxury at that time.[8]

He introduced the girls to good strong literature. Instead of 'hymns for Sundays and pretty bits for weekdays' he read to them Scott's 'Marmion' and Browning's 'Saul', then Wordsworth's and Tennyson's poetry. Through him they came to see the poverty of their attitude to religion. Angela wrote of his effect on the family:

> He came not a conventional youth, with polite smooth talk, but like a prophet of old. Long before we thought of him as having any religious message to us, gradually we found he knew about everything and could put any difficulty right, be it to answer 'Is there a God?' or 'What is poetry?' or 'What about ghosts and fairies?'[9]

Thus he was, even in his early twenties, showing his wonderful ability to win people's confidence, to invite them to tell him their troubles, and to inspire them with hope.

Louisa Powell was the smallest of the family, with a good figure; in fact her slender waist was the object of some teasing from her brothers and sisters. When she became engaged they gave her various samples of verse, all on the topic of her waist:

> You know that our Lou has grown graceful and slender;
> Like the breeze on the aspen, a zephyr may bend her!
> Is it squeezing and pulling, and tugging and pressing
> With steel and with whalebone, with jean and with lacing?
> Oh, no! but give ear and the reason I'll tell
> Why a finger and thumb her waist may span well:
> She has lost her large heart, and there's nothing within
> But back-bone and ribs, nerves, muscles and skin.[10]

She never, in fact, wore stays. Photographs show her with a rather large mouth, but with expressive eyes and long hands. She had a bright sense of humour and was always ready to see the ridiculous in people and situations: humbug did not last long with her. Although she was two years older than George (she was born on 5 November 1822), he was attracted to her more than to any of her sisters, and eventually he married her. Her family originated from South Wales, and it may be that a strong development of Celtic sensitivity in her made her particularly sympathetic to him. About June 1846 he began to write to her from Fulham, addressing her by her Christian name and taking advantage of his relationship with her sister-in-law to sign himself 'your affectionate cousin'.

His letters from this time show less tendency to introspection and a more confident optimism. No doubt he found in Louisa Powell a support and encouragement that perhaps even she herself was ignorant of. In later years Greville was to suggest that her musical abilities impressed his father greatly, and were important throughout their married life in encouraging and supporting him: 'Her pure and rich mezzo-soprano voice had been finely trained, and its tenderness did much, I think, to encourage her husband's genius.'[11] At about this time George made for his stepmother a pair of slippers in wool-work, done in cross-stitch, representing acorns and leaves in green with a scarlet background. Louisa must have taught him this particular craft, his aptitude for and interest in handicrafts giving him a fine opportunity to be with her. In the letter accompanying the gift to his mother (he never thought or spoke of her as 'stepmother') he said,

> I can sew very well now—always mend my own clothes—use my thimble—a nice silver one—like a lady. I have patched my trousers two or three times—an accomplishment I have attained since I came to England, and a most useful one I find it to be![12]

In July 1846 he sent Louisa a poem he had written, adding tactlessly but honestly that he had intended to give it to Helen, and thinks that he might have done so (although in fact he had not). Louisa wrote at the foot of it the words 'My Dear, my Dearest!' and adds in a fit of unselfconfidence, 'I am an overgrown baby with manners like a bear vexed!'[13] Of course, she was jealous of her sister-in-law and of the close relationship she had with George. Louisa felt that Helen set a standard of beauty and accomplishment that she could not attain to. She wanted to be 'fascinating' as Helen was, and felt intensely her failure, as she thought it, in this direction.

George was probably, at this stage, unaware of Louisa's need for reassurance. In any case it was impossible for him to begin to think of marrying Louisa while he was living as a tutor in Fulham. Late in the spring of 1848 he resigned his situation with some relief. He had found it very difficult to keep his temper sometimes, for he was sensitive, as only a Celt can be, to implied or imagined insults. His sense of humour probably helped him to a certain extent, but he had found the best answer for him lay in his natural inclination to regard life and experience from a personal religious standpoint. His tutorship was a trial through which he had to go, a struggle to vanquish resentment and to learn patience and forbearance. Now he wrote to Louisa,

> The difficulties with which I told you I was surrounded are not the results of my situation. However ill I may bear them at times, I regard my trials here as helps, not hindrances. But my difficulties are those which a heart far from God must feel, even when the hand of the Heavenly Father is leading it back to himself. It seems a wonder that he can bear with me.[14]

MacDonald had been thinking more and more seriously of becoming a minister. He had written candidly to his father, telling him exactly what he felt and thought about it:

> I do not wish you to understand me as having finally made up my mind as to the ministry. 'Tis true this feeling has been gradually gaining ground on me. What a mercy I was not allowed to follow out Chemistry! But, on the other hand, I fear myself—I have so much vanity, so much pride ... I have not prayed much about it, for it has seemed so far in the distance, as if it was scarcely time to think of it yet ... I love my Bible more—I am always finding out something new in it. All my teaching in youth seems useless to me. I must get it all from the Bible again ... If the Gospel of Jesus be not true, I can only pray my maker to annihilate me, for nothing else is worth living for; and if that be true, everything in the universe is glorious, except sin ... One of my greatest difficulties in consenting to think of religion was that I thought I should have to give up my beautiful thoughts and my love for the things God has made. But I find that the happiness springing from all things not in themselves sinful is much increased by religion. God is the God of the Beautiful, Religion the love of the Beautiful, and Heaven the home of the Beautiful, Nature is tenfold brighter in the sun of Righteousness, and my love of Nature is more intense since I became a Christian—if indeed I am one. God had not given me such thoughts and forbidden me to enjoy them.[15]

On the face of it it seems strange that MacDonald could, in the same letter, seriously discuss entering the ministry, and yet doubt his being a Christian at all. However, his doubts should not be taken to indicate a lack of faith. He was doubting himself; he had since leaving Aberdeen discovered his own vanity and pride, and now had a sense of his own unworthiness. His father could have written to him pointing out that such self-doubt never debarred anyone from being a Christian; indeed, according to Christ's story of the Prodigal Son, who came home saying 'Father, I am no more worthy to be called your son', it is a prerequisite to being accepted by God. MacDonald's divergence on points of doctrine from the Aberdeenshire Calvinists did not in itself mean that he was not a Christian. After all, his London pastor, Dr Morison, also differed from them. MacDonald's independence of thought was leading him to a more exalted experience of God than old Dr Kennedy could possibly comprehend.

For it is clear from this letter to his father that MacDonald's personal faith was becoming most important to him. He was finding that it informed and enriched his whole mental life and enabled him to appreciate things not in themselves connected with religion. However, it is significant that his spiritual experience lay only in the realm of 'the Beautiful' and 'Nature', not in human relationships. He had not learned how to deal with people like his employers at Fulham, and this could be a serious drawback to a minister. Yes, he could feel he was drawing closer to God and learning new, exciting truths which he could pass on to a congregation—but how would he manage on the pastoral side? His inner spirituality was not yet sufficient to help him to encounter superficial, self-centred religiosity.

A theological college course would not help him much in this respect, either. Pastoral and clinical training was scarcely touched on in the nineteenth century, emphasis being all on preaching and doctrine. MacDonald needed his father's advice as to whether or not he should enter a college, and returned home to Huntly for the summer of 1848. As his father would be paying his fees, his consent was essential. He also wished to ask his approval of his choice of Louisa Powell for his future wife. He had little doubt of obtaining this: he once said that he 'had never asked his father for anything, as boy or man, but it was given'[16]—a comment that says as much about MacDonald as about his father. He had missed his home with its winds, its hills and its rivers, but even more was he longing to see his mother and his new sister Jane. He had a thoroughly enjoyable holiday, and must have been in particularly good health, for his mother later used to tell how she saw him pick up his two youngest sisters, aged four and two years, and with one under each arm race around the house and leap over a hedge. His friend Robert Troup, who was eventually to become the Congregational minister at Huntly, was home on holiday too, after his first year at Highbury Theological College. MacDonald and Louisa seem to have agreed not to correspond during this summer; at any rate, no letters passed between them.

With his father's encouragement MacDonald went back to London in September to enter Highbury College. He chose this college because he already had a few friends there, including, of course, Robert Troup. Shortly after his entry to the College he wrote a formal letter to Mr Powell, asking to be accepted as Louisa's fiancé. Although he had no money and not much prospect of becoming rich (ministers' pay was notoriously low), he was accepted. It may be that Mr and Mrs Powell were persuaded by the winning quality in his character. They must have hoped that as poet and prophet he had a bright future ahead of him.

*

MacDonald made few friends at Highbury College, partly because most of the students were greatly his inferior in intellect. As MA he had to study for only two years, instead of the usual four; and in fact he himself initiated lectures to the other students on chemistry and natural philosophy, thus continuing the interest he had formed at Aberdeen. He was a member of the Debating Society, and when a paper was read on 'The Aesthetics of Public Worship' he supported its condemnation of the bad taste and unnatural sentiment in dissenting chapels. Life in the College was much more comfortable than in the hurly-burly of Aberdeen; each student had his own study and bedroom, and they took their meals together, being for that reason much better fed than some of the poor students in Scotland. They met together every morning and evening for Bible reading and prayer.

He did make one very dear friend, the brother of his fellow-student James Matheson.[17] Greville Ewing Matheson worked as a bank clerk and lived with his widowed mother in Islington, not far from the College. Her home was open to any friend of her sons, and her hospitality was very welcome to George MacDonald. The admiration and criticism of Greville Matheson meant a great deal to him, and in later years he was to include his friend's poetry in the collection of poems *A Threefold Cord*. A third brother, William, often joined the group of friends; they would go to concerts together, to art exhibitions at the National Gallery, and occasionally to the theatre.

The theatre at that period was in a very poor state, both artistically and morally, and respectable people avoided it. However, George MacDonald had a great love for drama, particularly that of Shakespeare, and he was not afraid of other people's opinions. After one visit to the theatre he received an anonymous letter which advised him 'that he had been closely observed by a well-wisher, who, if such promptings of Satan were ever yielded to again, would secure his expulsion from Highbury. But some trick in the penmanship revealed the perpetrator of the joke to be one of his companions in the iniquity.'[18] Presumably it was either Greville or William Matheson.

The Mathesons were soon introduced to The Limes; MacDonald asked Louisa to call on Mrs Matheson, which she did, although she was shy and diffident on such occasions. The call was followed up with formal invitations to a charade party at The Limes, and thereafter the Mathesons were often to be seen with the Powells. They would sometimes go on expeditions with George and the Powells to Greenwich or Richmond. MacDonald was an excellent horseman, and this was a point in his favour with old Mr Powell, who would often lend him a mount so that he could accompany one or more of his daughters on a round of calls.

Another friend made at Highbury was his Professor of Systematic Theology and New Testament Exegesis, John Godwin. As he was the only professor to live at the College, he was regarded as its Principal. His approach to the New Testament was considered by the rigorous as rather unorthodox. He believed that man has the ability and the responsibility to choose whether or not he will be saved. MacDonald was indebted to him for his exposition of the New Testament.

Despite Godwin's disapproval MacDonald occasionally went to hear the liberal thinker A. J. Scott lecturing at the Marylebone Institute, and so formed an acquaintance that was to stand him in good stead in later years. Alexander John Scott had begun his career as a minister in Paisley. However, he began to associate himself with those who rejected Calvin-

31

ism, and with the Irvingite Charismatic renewal of the nineteenth century. He claimed that the Holy Spirit of God could if invoked play a more prominent part in Christians' lives. He advocated 'speaking in tongues' as the Apostles did on the Day of Pentecost, and spiritual healing.[19] He was invited to take a post as minister in Woolwich, but declared himself unable to subscribe any longer to the Westminster Confession. His licence as a minister was revoked. His intellectual gifts were recognised in other circles, however, and by the time MacDonald was studying at Highbury Scott had become Professor of English Language and Literature at University College London. His 'liberality' consisted in this, that he proclaimed the love of God the Father, the universality of Christ's redemption, and the availability of the Holy Spirit to all men. MacDonald was finding friendship and encouragement from men whose ideas were along the same lines as his own.

It is hard to tell how much he gained from his theological course. He benefited, no doubt, from the opportunity to study the New Testament closely in its original Greek, and to read the classical works of theology apart from those of Calvin and his disciples. Though he studied Irenaeus, Augustine and Luther, among others, he began to feel that scholarship alone in the interpretation of Christ's words was worthless if not positively dangerous. In his later writings he was to lay great emphasis on the need for a heart in tune with God for a right interpretation of the Scriptures.

A large part of the training at Highbury concentrated on preaching, this being the heart of the Nonconformist ministry. Professor Godwin was critical of MacDonald's preaching, saying that he was too informal in his manner, that he tended to be too intellectual and poetical in his expositions, and that he was doctrinally insecure. Nevertheless he found many preaching engagements for him—these were important for the students as a means of gaining experience—and had to admit that he generally gave satisfaction to his hearers.

In June 1849 MacDonald went to Cork for three months as temporary pastor. This was something of a vacation job, as although he would be earning money, he still had to complete his course at Highbury. The extended period of his stay would give him valuable experience of a pastor's work. He was naturally sorry to leave Louisa, but he felt that God's work must come first.

The Irish welcomed him hospitably, and one of the deacons lent him a horse so that his stay was even more pleasurable. Yet he still suffered from bronchitis and consequent low spirits—something he had been enduring on and off throughout his Highbury career. A letter written to his father gives some idea of the sort of life he led in Ireland:

> I am very glad I came here, to let me try myself a little; and though I have not so much confidence in my capabilities as perhaps you have, yet I get on pretty well, tho' I am very doubtful how I shall ever be able to write more than one sermon a week... Yesterday morning I went some six miles east from Youghal to see the devotions of the poor Catholics at one of the round towers of Ireland... They want me to go to Killarney before I leave, and indeed I should be sorry to leave without seeing those lakes; but, though I think this is more valuable than many a book that you would quite approve of my laying out the money for, I don't know what you will say to it...
>
> By the way, the Queen was here last Friday. I didn't see her—for I am no worshipper of royalty ... I believe there was no great enthusiasm amongst the lower classes—how could there be!—but she was received with every possible demonstration of loyalty—a great deal more show than I was pleased with, considering the state of the country.[20]

The letters that passed between George and Louisa during these three months show that Louisa was beginning to feel a strong sense of the greatness of her fiancé and of his exalted relation with God, and a consequent sense of her own unworthiness to be his wife. She was oppressed by her inability to share in his joys over God's glories and wrote saying that she was unfit, that he should let her go, that she could bear anything that was good for him. Her jealousy of Helen had lessened with her formal engagement, but she still felt that she was not good enough for George. Her letters were not all self-deprecating, however. She shared her thoughts and feelings with him, her appreciation of a new book or poem, or described in witty and even satirical terms people that she had met. She related to him a dream that she had; it is worth recording because it is surely prophetic in its foreshadowing of a photograph taken of George and Louisa on their golden wedding anniversary:

> I was looking earnestly at the clouds when one thick volume of pink and white cloud had two faces ... I looked at them for a long time not knowing who it was, but soon discerned your face, only grown into a beautiful old man with the most glorified and perfectly beautiful expression upon it. The other for some time I thought was Mama, but upon looking and thinking, hoped it was I, with long white hair. I held a book out of which you were reading. You had your arm round my neck ... I dreamt that, after looking for some time, the cloud melted away; then someone told me it was a vision sent to me that I might not fear present evil to either of us.[21]

Although she was certain of her love for George, she did not always write of it, which caused MacDonald to ask whether she was 'taking a rest from loving him'—to which she replied earnestly,

> I think, rather, that my not expressing it would arise from the calmness and repose which the confidence of loving you and possessing your love gives me. Now I am sure I have been improper enough even for you! But I could not bear you to think I *rested* from that same! How often when I am writing to you I wish I could just look into your face to see what you think about it, to see if I have said anything that would at all displease you.[22]

While he was at Cork MacDonald made his first attempt at growing a beard, and returned to London with a neat growth on his chin. At that time beards were frowned upon not only because they were considered dirty, but also because they were supposed to hark back to the savage and heathenish days of mankind. MacDonald was thwarted in his attempt to grow one by his prospective father-in-law (he was staying at The Limes before returning to Highbury). Greville records that

> when Mr Powell returned from the city and found him in the drawing-room with his daughters, he hesitated for one moment, gave him a second look, then, without greeting, turned and left the

room. My father, so my mother would tell us, immediately went to his own room and, with soap and a razor, obliterated his offence.[23]

The lovers had to separate again, as Louisa had to go to Lynmouth in Devon with her sisters and her mother, who was recovering from a serious haemorrhage. MacDonald settled down to his studies at Highbury. He was now preaching at various churches not so much to gain experience as to try and gain a permanent post. Congregational ministers were appointed by the congregation after an initial trial period. George wrote to his father telling him of a disappointment at Stebbing:

> a note came from one of the deacons at Stebbing, telling me that I had better not go, as I was not acceptable to many of the people... The more intellectual part, I believe, would have liked me to go—indeed, I think that is the feeling about me generally in other places; [but] many say they can't understand me. I tried to be as simple as possible at Stebbing... Perhaps my manner is too quiet to please dissenters commonly. However, I must not do violence to the nature God has given me and put anything on. I think, if people will try, I can make them understand me—if they won't, I have no desire to be understood. I can't do their part of the work.[24]

His brother Charles was now a deacon in a fashionable Manchester chapel, and wrote urging him to join him; with his influence, he said, George could get the post of assistant to his minister, with a salary of £200 per annum. This was an extremely generous offer; as a minister MacDonald might reasonably have expected £150, although some clergymen had to struggle along on as little as £50. But neither George nor Louisa was attracted to Manchester as yet, and they knew that Charles's optimism was sometimes ill-founded. Instead George went to Whitehaven in Cumbria for a month's trial. In one letter to his father he asked what salary he should expect. His father replied,

> As to ministers' stipends in general, they are in most cases but too small.... It requires *much prudence* on the part of *any* minister, whether old or young, when necessity compels him to bring his own necessities before the church. Not a few who would hug to their bosom the *poor starveling*, would dash him from them to

35

be trampled underfoot when ... an increased stipend was needed! ... I hope you will by and by be in circumstance to pay off your small debts, and make conscience of never venturing on taking a wife before then.[25]

The Whitehaven trial came to nothing, and MacDonald returned to Highbury. Louisa's mother died in June 1850; the Powells felt in need of a holiday, and for the months of August and September Mr Powell rented a house in Brighton. He himself travelled into London every day for business, in spite of his age—he was seventy. At the same time MacDonald went to Trinity Congregational Church in Arundel as temporary pastor—a not too inconvenient place for visiting Brighton. It soon looked as if he would be invited to stay on permanently— a pleasing prospect for both him and Louisa.

3

The young minister 1850–3

MacDonald found Arundel very pleasant. It was less beautiful than Huntly, though the surrounding countryside was lusher. The two towns were similar in size and both were situated on rivers, with surrounding hills; but the South Downs were to the highlander's eye 'very low hills'. The Arun provided transport to and from the coast, but even with the commerce fostered by sizeable boats, 'it is a very quiet little town—not so much bustle as Huntly.'[1] The people of Trinity Church were simple and eager to learn, mainly tradesmen with a few who came in from the country round about. It was not a long-established church; there was still alive an old lady who had been active in its formation. In 1850 it had sixty-two members.

The two towns, Huntly and Arundel, could be seen as representative of two contrasting elements in MacDonald's life. Huntly typifies the Scottish compound of Celtic vision and Calvinist dourness which had formed his spiritual outlook; and Arundel the new life he was just beginning among ordinary, rather commonplace and often irritating English men and women. His work was henceforth to be one of service to such people, preaching and teaching, trying to bring enlightenment and improvement to their lives. The Arundel experience was to show him how difficult it could be for one coming from the heights of spiritual experience to accommodate himself to the 'very low hills'—the shallow superficiality of South-of-England religiosity.[2]

At the beginning things went well. MacDonald preached as a 'supply'—a temporary pastor—for two months in the late summer of 1850. The Powells occasionally rode over from Brighton to see him. Louisa came for a day at the end of August, accompanied by her sister Charlotte and her sister-in-law Helen. Then the following Sunday her father brought her over and they attended worship at Trinity Church. Before breakfast the next day the old man wrote a long letter to the young minister, giving him plenty of advice. Such a letter might easily have been patronising, but this was rather apologetic and respectful in its tone. He thought MacDonald's reading of the Scriptures was good, 'because you avoided monotony by giving the emphasis natural to the various speakers in the narrative parts'. For himself, however, he inclined to the view of his 'illustrious friend', Samuel Taylor Coleridge, that the Scriptures 'should be delivered more as the Oracles of God than the opinions of man'.[3] George's reading was not grand enough for Mr Powell.

By the end of September Trinity Church had made up its mind in George's favour, and on 3 October the church meeting decided to make him the formal offer of a permanent pastorate, at a salary of £150 per annum. He wrote 'in great haste and half-dressed' to his father the following day to tell him the good news:

> I expect to find the work of preaching grow easier and easier, but will be oppressed at first, I fear. That will teach me more faith . . . I will send you some of my poetry and a sermon or two soon; for [at present] I have not time to spend on the composition of sermons, which I preach in a very different style from that in which I write them.[4]

He was also approached by a church in Brighton, who wished to have him as their minister. This would have given him a higher salary, with a congregation that was well-to-do and better educated than that at Arundel. But he preferred the simpler, more affectionate style of the smaller church, and believed that his Lord was leading him to Arundel rather than Brighton. By the end of October he was settling down in his lodgings and in the church.

> My congregation I think increases [he wrote to his father] and the week meetings on the whole are better. We have a prayer-meeting every Monday, and a lecture on Thursday, for which I do not make much preparation—but gather up the gleanings of the Sunday. I mean on those same evenings to have Bible classes, one

for young men and the other for young women. I shall have plenty to do ... I hope to be able to visit a good deal amongst the poor and unwell.[5]

There was the question of ordination to be settled. In most denominations this was done when the minister took up his first post. MacDonald himself felt that the 'call' of the congregation itself constituted his ordination—a view that was to become more generally accepted in Congregational Churches. But some of the members of Trinity Church had views of a more sacramental nature. They felt that their pastor could not properly administer Holy Communion until some rite of ordination had been performed. MacDonald did not feel strongly in the matter; he therefore arranged that his friend the Rev Caleb Morris should officiate at an ordination service at the end of November,

Now that MacDonald could support a wife the wedding could be fixed for the following spring and a visit to Huntly planned as a honeymoon. First, however, George had a particular favour to ask of Louisa. Helen Powell possessed several notebooks containing George's early attempts at poetry. Now he wanted Louisa to have them, and he wanted Helen to know that he and Louisa kept nothing secret from one another. So he asked his fiancée to get the books from her sister-in-law. He hoped that this would restore good relations between the two women.

> I went to Helen's last night [wrote Louisa to George] ... She pretended not to know what I meant at first ... However, she soon understood me, and when I asked for them, saying Papa would perhaps take them, she said, 'Very well, Louisa, I will make up a little packet for *him*.' ... She was very pleasant and more natural than sometimes, I think, and so we were more cordial friends. I should not like her to go away with all the uncomfortable feeling that I am sure has existed on both sides ... I hope your pocket-books have not shared the fate of the poetry she told me was for no eyes but her own and was therefore put on the fire.[6]

The episode seems to have laid to rest the demon of jealousy. Helen went on a visit to Banff, and Louisa found herself fully occupied in making shirts and a stock-cravat for her beloved before she could turn her attention to her own wedding dress. Her twenty-eighth birthday was on 5 November, and many of her presents were 'housekeepingish'. But her sister Angela gave her a chain knitted from George's hair, so that she could wear him around her neck. George himself gave her Tennyson's 'In Memoriam,' copied out in his beautiful handwriting.

The mood of optimism and expectancy was not to last. George was seized with a severe haemorrhage of the lungs, and all plans were postponed. At first Mr Powell feared it was a sign that his daughter was not meant to marry George MacDonald. 'No, Papa!' exclaimed Louisa; 'it is a sign that I must marry him at once and nurse him!' When a letter came from Arundel with reassuring news of an improvement in MacDonald's condition, he began to believe that his daughter was right. She was not allowed to nurse him on this occasion, though; it would hardly be proper, they said. But her brother Alex went to Arundel for the weekend and brought back news of a continued improvement in the patient's condition. MacDonald had to lie on his back with leeches on his chest, but was able to scribble little notes for Alex to take back to London.

By November he was well enough to go up to London for a consultation with Dr C. J. B. Williams, who diagnosed tuberculosis of the lungs. He ordered his patient not to preach for at least six weeks, and prescribed cod-liver oil. MacDonald himself was not alarmed by this pronouncement. He felt that his trouble was slight, and that proper care would set him right for this occasion—although he knew that the haemorrhage was liable to attack again. He was disappointed to be laid low before he had fairly got going in his ministry, but, as with his previous troubles as a tutor, he tried to understand the present difficulty from a religious point of view. God had a plan for his life, a plan of which love was the basis. 'There is a reason, and I at least shall be the better for it,'[7] he wrote to his father. In this letter he told of Dr Williams's verdict and asked for advice as to what he should do. He had spent a lot of money on books—a necessary expenditure, he felt, in a place like Arundel where he could expect to meet few people of any intelligence, and none with any books he could borrow. He thought that Trinity Church would not seek another minister, and would wait for him to recover; but the 'pulpit supplies'—stand-in ministers—were paid at the rate of £2 per week out of MacDonald's salary. This left him with very little money to pay for his own convalescence.

His father was very disturbed at the news, and wrote anxious but encouraging letters from Huntly. He arranged with his sister, Mary Spence, that George should convalesce at her home on the Isle of Wight. He had good food—plus his cod-liver oil—plenty of rest and some gentle exercise. Although he was not supposed to be working, he could not be idle. He began and completed a dramatic poem in five acts, *Within and Without*. He dedicated it to Louisa with a poem beginning 'Receive thine own, for I and it are thine'.[8] He had learned from Louisa during their courtship that husband and wife need to share their spiritual life. In *Within and Without* the young wife Lilia fears she is losing her husband's love. He is in fact too involved in his own search for God to give her the signs of love she needs. MacDonald would make sure such a thing did not happen in his own marriage.

At the beginning of January 1851 MacDonald went up to London to visit the Powells and to see Dr Williams. The doctor declared him fit for work. More important, the wedding plans could go ahead. Saturday 8 March was the chosen day. Mac-Donald returned to Arundel on 16 January and from there completed plans for the wedding in correspondence with Louisa. The Huntly trip had to be cancelled because Scotland would be too cold for the invalid in early spring; Louisa's two maiden aunts, the Misses Sharman, came to the rescue and offered their house in Leamington for the honeymoon.

On 3 March George went to stay with the Mathesons in London; his brother Alec was there too. His other brother John was teaching in Sheffield and unable to get away even for the wedding itself. He hoped to see the newly-weds in May, when he was expecting to visit the Great Exhibition. The wedding took place at the Old Gravel Pits Chapel, Hackney. Old Mr Powell had urgent business in Bristol, and was afraid he would not be able to return in time for the wedding; but he made it and brought with him a beautiful white stole for the bride to wear. At the most solemn moment of the ceremony

Louisa noticed a shop-ticket on one corner of the stole, and had great difficulty in suppressing her laughter.

MacDonald's wedding present to his bride was a poem, 'Love me, Beloved'. In it he considered the sorrows that might lie in store for them, particularly the sorrow of being divided in death, but concludes triumphantly:

> Love me, beloved; Hades and Death
> Shall vanish away like a frosty breath;
> These hands, that now art at home in thine,
> Shall clasp thee again, if thou still art mine;
> And thou shalt be mine, my spirit's bride,
> In the ceaseless flow of eternity's tide,
> If the truest love that thy heart can know
> Meet the truest love that from mine can flow.
> Pray God, beloved, for thee and me,
> That our souls may be wedded eternally.[9]

The poem was later included in the published version of *Within and Without*.

The newly-weds went to Leamington via Rugby, where MacDonald had a preaching engagement for Sunday 9th. When they unpacked their luggage they found that George's bottle of cod-liver oil had broken and spilt all over his Sunday-best trousers!

As his married home MacDonald had chosen a little house in Tarrant Street, Arundel; Mr Powell had paid the rent and furnished it down to the last detail as a gift to the newly-wedded couple. When they returned from their honeymoon they settled down happily to their work with the congregation of Trinity Church. MacDonald was not at first very fit for work, and had to spare himself where he could. He felt that preaching, in particular, might bring on another attack. Louisa took a share in the pastoral visiting, and made many friends with her ready sympathy. George, too, had a wonderful gift of compassion, so that those in trouble could feel that he was sharing their anguish. The MacDonalds were greatly loved, particularly by the poor and uneducated.

George's limited experience as a preacher, combined with what he heard in other churches, made him incline strongly

42

towards extempore preaching. 'Most preaching seems to me greatly beside the mark,' he wrote to his father. 'That only can I prize which tends to make men better—and most of it "does na play bouf upo' me [doesn't even bark at me]."'[10] He was concerned that his congregation should be putting their faith into practice, and not just assenting to theories. He firmly believed that

> people have hitherto been a great deal too much taken up about doctrine and far too little about practice. The word *doctrine*, as used in the Bible, means teaching of duty, not theory. I preached a sermon about this. We are far too anxious to be definite and to have finished, well-polished, sharp-edged *systems*—forgetting that the more perfect a theory about the infinite, the surer it is to be wrong, the more impossible it is to be right. I am neither Arminian nor Calvinist. To no system would I subscribe.[11]

Arundel had its share of 'characters', and MacDonald drew on his experiences with them when he came to write his novel *Annals of a Quiet Neighbourhood*. The portrait of Old Rogers was taken directly from life. The real Old Rogers often appeared in the chapel in his round frock-coat, red cotton handkerchief and tall beaver hat. He had sailed in a man-of-war and was full of nautical similes. He would liken the pulpit to a crow's nest: 'I love a parson. . . . He's got a good telescope, and he gits to the mast-head, and he looks out. And he sings out, "Land ahead!" or "Breakers ahead!" and gives directions according'.[12]

The long-delayed ordination service took place in June 1851. Charlotte Powell came to help with the arrangements, and Professor Godwin was invited to officiate. Godwin, a childless widower, was immediately attracted to Charlotte, and two years later they were married, George MacDonald officiating on that occasion. Alec and John both attended the ordination, and took back an account to their father. He wrote to George, 'John and Alec are greatly delighted with Arundel and with the *minister's wife* thereof'.[13]

The young couple had plenty of visitors in Arundel. The Powell girls often came to stay, as did Greville Matheson. Occasionally MacDonald was able to take a trip to London. He and Greville Matheson would help each other with literary work. George and Louisa together made a book of Matheson's sonnets and poems, George copying them out and Louisa painting floral designs around each poem. George himself was working on a translation from the German of twelve of the *Spiritual Songs* of Novalis. He had this printed and gave copies to his friends as a Christmas present. The mystical piety of Novalis' poetry had gripped MacDonald in his student days, and now he shared its riches with others. One of his close friends at this time was T. T. Lynch, the hymn-writer, who acknowledged his copy with gratitude.

Another copy undoubtedly went to his youngest brother John, who was himself a poet of some genius. The two often debated the claims of unfettered imagination over stern discipline, both in poetry and in life. John, with his restless, nomadic instincts, lacked George's ability to harness his genius by sheer hard work. He did not stay long at his teaching job in Sheffield, though he was, as his brother said, 'a born teacher' and could have made a success anywhere. First he moved to a school in Manchester, then, in search of adventure, he took a post at a boys' school in Moscow. He was to enjoy a series of hair-raising adventures before returning to England. The love between him and George was very deep. George admired his young brother, and was to include a portrait of him as Ian MacRuadh in *What's Mine's Mine*, and as Eric Ericsen in *Robert Falconer*. He would include some of John's poems in these books, and others in *A Threefold Cord*.

On the 4 January 1852 George and Louisa's first child was born. It was a girl, and her parents named her Lilia Scott: Lilia after the girl in *Within and Without*, and Scott after A. J. Scott, whose lectures in London MacDonald remembered with gratitude and admiration. Many years later Louisa was to write of '. . . exultant joys, blissful, ecstatic delights—such as we both had when first holding and gazing on Lilia—that White Wonder!'[14]

John wrote from Manchester congratulating George and Louisa. In the same letter he shared his concern over the middle brother, Alec, who was employed there as a salesman. Alec, now twenty-four, had not the intellect of George and

44

John. His versifying was limited to humorous doggerel, but he had inherited his grandmother's business acumen, and was doing well in his work. John was worried about how Alec would take a disappointment in love: 'he does not seem to entertain much hope and he is very sad and looking ill, though perfectly quiet and patient.'[15]

The lady did eventually respond to Alec's love, and for a while they were happy, but Alec began to spit blood, and tuberculosis of the lungs was diagnosed. In March he went to Arundel to be nursed, and found some comfort in Louisa's sympathy. However, Arundel's climate did not suit his condition, and he wanted to be at home in Huntly. He went there in the summer. His health did not improve, and his girl-friend's father, probably guessing that Alec was dying, put an end to the relationship. Alec wrote to Louisa,

> I told her long ago that it was 'better to have loved and lost than never to have loved at all'. I can say so still ... I do not blame her, she could not help it ... I have no further claim. I cannot wish to forget her, but my hopes can fold their wings now, for it is winter, and for a time at least they must rest. My fears are dead.[16]

In April 1853 Alec died in his father's arms.

George had not been able to visit Huntly, but the oldest brother, Charles, had managed to see Alec just before he died. The dying man had comforted the living: 'Never mind, Charles, man,' he said. 'This is nae the end o' it!' George wrote to his father, 'Of him we need never say he *was*; for what he was he is now—only expanded, enlarged and glorified. He needed no change, only development.'[17]

1852 had been a difficult year, not only on account of Alec MacDonald's troubles, but also because of a rift that was showing itself in the congregation of Trinity Church. To the poor, MacDonald showed himself thoroughly sympathetic and selfless; he preached with equal thoroughness against the worship of mammon, against cruelty and self-seeking. He offended the rich, and he knew it. 'The few young who are ... not influenced by their parents', he wrote to his father, 'and the simple, honest poor are much attached to me ...' and in another letter, '*some* of all classes *do* understand me, and I am

happy not to be understood by those who do not understand... Some say I talk foolishness, others go away with
their hearts burning within them.'[18]

Criticisms were being made about his orthodoxy as well as
about his preaching. His relaxed attitude to keeping the Sabbath offended those who wanted to make it a dreary alter-
nation of church attendance with doing nothing. In addition
he caused an outrage among certain elderly ladies by suggesting that the animals might be sharers in the life after death. On
both these points MacDonald was felt to be 'unScriptural'
(and therefore unorthodox). He may not have been scrupulous
in keeping to the letter of certain Scriptures, but he was following the spirit of such texts as 'The Sabbath was made for man
and not man for the Sabbath', and 'The creation itself will be
set free from its bondage to decay and obtain the glorious
liberty of the children of God.'

His landlord, the richest and most influential of the deacons,
could not bear to think that such a respectable person as himself might be harbouring a heretic. He hinted to MacDonald
that he should look around for another house, suggesting as an
excuse that MacDonald's present accommodation was too
small for his needs. In June matters came to a head. The
deacons made a deputation to their minister and proposed
to reduce his salary. Their pretext was that as he was seeking
a larger house his salary must be over-generous! MacDonald
was finding it hard enough to make ends meet, but he knew his
affairs were in God's hands. This enabled him to acquiesce
gracefully. The deacons, dumbfounded, stuttered and stam-
mered for quite some time. Finally the landlord blurted out,
'We thought you would take it as a hint—your preaching is not
acceptable—we want you to resign.'

They had two particular charges against him. One was that
in a sermon he had suggested that some provision is made for
the heathen after death. The other was that he was tainted
with German theology. The new liberal theology, with its new
ways of approaching biblical interpretation, was coming into
Britain from Germany; as a result conservative churchmen
were suspicious of anything that smelt of 'Germanism'. Mac-
Donald did take an interest in 'higher criticism' and had an

open mind towards it; but it is most likely that what upset the deacons of Trinity Church was his translation of Novalis' poems. They were an expression of German religion, and that was enough for the deacons.

Although it was within their rights to reduce his salary (for his final half-year they paid him £56 16s), MacDonald would not resign at their behest. He referred the matter to the church-meeting. He put it to the church that 'as I came at the invitation of the whole church, it would be unfair to the other members of the church to resign unconditionally on account of the dissatisfaction of a few.'[19] He wished to know whether the church as a whole sympathised with the critics. A proposition was put before the meeting:

> We do not by any means sympathise with the statement which has been made that 'there is nothing in his preaching.' But we do sympathise with those who were dissatisfied with the statement from the pulpit 'that with the Heathen the time of trial does not (in his, the Revd G. MacDonald's opinion) cease at their death', which certainly implies a future state of probation. And this church considers such a view is not in accordance with the Scriptures and quite differs with the sentiments held by the ministers of the Independent Denomination.[20]

Only about twenty members agreed to this proposition, and MacDonald refused to resign. Nor did he retract the statement that had given offence. He had found the deacons' attitude particularly galling, and shared his annoyance with his father:

> I have been very much occupied with some annoyance given me by some members of the church who are very unteachable. I thought it not unlikely at the time that I should have to leave. . . . If God put the means at any time in my power, I mean to take another mode of helping men; and no longer stand in this position towards them, in which they regard you more as *their* servant than as Christ's.[21]

George and Louisa had to struggle on as best they could; and now they discovered their true friends. The poorer members of the church would send all sorts of gifts—fruit and vegetables, home-brewed beer—and even, when their pastor was ill, delicacies such as custards and chicken that they could never afford for themselves. Louisa wished to add to the family income by taking in three or four little girls and giving them 'a good English education, with music and the rudiments of French, Italian and German,' for £60 per annum. She advertised accordingly, but no pupils came. It was perhaps just as well, with Lilia growing rapidly and another baby on the way.

In May 1853 MacDonald resigned. Feelings were running higher than ever, both for and against him. Rather than have a divided church, he decided to leave.

4

The Manchester experience 1853–6

The question was, what to do next? MacDonald had made his decision knowing it would be difficult to find another post. Trinity Church was not likely to give him good references. The baby was due in about nine weeks, and Louisa really needed to stay in Arundel. The couple decided that Louisa should stay where she was until after the baby was born, while George should go at once to Manchester to seek a post.

An ugly, smoky industrial centre seems an odd choice for one prone to tuberculosis, but Manchester had overriding attractions for MacDonald. To begin with he had made visits while his three brothers were living there, and had met people whose minds were alert and who were active in pursuit of God's truth. The mental atmosphere of Manchester was as fresh air compared with the heaviness and stupidity of the Arundel deacons. By May Alec was dead and John was at Huntly preparing for his Russian trip, but Charles was still living in Radnor Street and George knew he could stay with him while he was looking for work.

Another attraction of Manchester was the presence there of A. J. Scott. He was appointed Principal of Owen's College (which was eventually to become Manchester University) in 1851. Scott had little ability as a writer, so his thought is largely unknown today. His influence in his lifetime sprang from exceptional gifts as a preacher and lecturer. MacDonald considered him the greatest intellect he had known. Scott would lecture without notes on such far-ranging subjects as vernacular literature, socialism, Chartism and the ballot-box, or church history, 'pouring out his immense learning in appeal to mind and heart such as few can ever have rivalled'.[1]

Shortly after his arrival in Manchester, MacDonald called

on Professor Scott and told him of his troubles. Scott's under-standing and encouragement did a great deal to raise the morale of the penniless MacDonald. He was always welcome in the Scotts' home, and met there others whose friendship, like that of the Scotts, was to be a support and comfort during the difficulties that lay ahead. It is possible that MacDonald's growing intimacy with this great charismatic figure helped him to see God at work in human affairs. Superficial, self-centred, commonplace people were still a problem to him. In fact, after his bitter experience he was even less ready to look for the good in them. Manchester might be a centre for liberal intellectuals, but it also contained many people whose attitudes were those of Arundel all over again. MacDonald was only too ready to despise this type of person. Church-going was becom-ing a burden to him for this reason, as he wrote to his father:

> As to the congregational meetings and my absence from them, per-haps if you saw a little behind the scenes you would care less for both. I will not go where I have not the slightest interest in going, and where my contempt would be excited to a degree very injuri-ous to myself.[2]

Scott could appreciate MacDonald's impatience with the Manchester Christians and with his Arundel deacons, especially as he himself had been deprived of a pulpit in simi-lar fashion. He may have talked to his younger friend about his belief in God's Holy Spirit, who works with infinite patience in even the most hidebound of conventional Christians. And did he tell MacDonald about his early days with the Irvingites, when invocation of and submission to the Spirit brought about an amazing liberation and dynamism in worship? Certainly, in his novel *The Seaboard Parish* MacDonald was to write with a certain wistfulness of prophetic utterance and spiritual free-dom in worship.[3]

Meanwhile Louisa was preparing for her confinement, with her sisters Carrie and Angela taking it in turns to look after her. They were kind enough to pay as boarders when they stayed in Arundel, thus helping the MacDonald finances. Mary Josephine was born on 23 July. Old Mr Powell was no doubt delighted with his second granddaughter, although he was not so pleased with his son-in-law. He and his other son-in-law, John Godwin, felt that MacDonald had been a bit too stubborn and high-minded; he could have kept his post at Arundel if he had been a bit more conciliating, and given the people preaching that was more suited to their tastes and abilities. But MacDonald believed that he must tell the truth as he saw it; he would not compromise the Gospel for the sake of his own security. Even if there was an element of stubbornness and pride in his attitude, his belief was entirely right, and its corollary, that he must trust to God for his material needs, was in line with Christ's highest teaching. 'You must not be surprised if you hear that I am not what is called *getting on*,' he wrote to his father. 'Time will show what use the Father will make of me. I desire to be His—entirely—so sure am I that therein lies all things. If less than this were my hope, I should die.'[4]

He guessed that he would have the same problem in Manchester as at Arundel if he was appointed by a Congregational chapel, and began to have hopes of gathering around himself a totally independent church. He attended chapel services in Manchester at first, but became even more disgusted with them. Much of the preaching consisted of apologies for money-making rather than preaching of the Gospel. By the Gospel MacDonald meant the account of Jesus' life and death as told by the Evangelists in the New Testament. He was not interested in any theological 'plan of salvation' but in the loveliness of the man, Christ Jesus. He felt that the contemporary emphasis on Christ's divinity set him at a distance. A study of the Gospels showed Jesus as a man, living, working and dying among men to bring them to his Father.

In September the post of librarian to Owen's College became vacant, and MacDonald applied for it—unsuccessfully. At such a time he particularly missed Louisa, although Charles and his wife Jane were very kind to him. The fact of his poverty was brought home to him at the beginning of October, when the deacons said that a quarter's rent for the house in Arundel had not been paid. The furniture had been put in store and Louisa was ready to go with the two little girls to her brother Alex's home in Liverpool. Louisa and George had both thought that all debts were settled, so this demand was something of a blow to them. George found the money somehow and sent it to Louisa, writing,

> I hope it will not trouble my sweet wife. It has done me a real good, I think; for even in poverty like ours, one is so much more ready to trust in what oneself has, than in what God has ready to give when needed.[5]

And in a later letter,

> Oh, dearest, whatever you feel about our homeless condition at present, I hope it has helped to teach your husband some things... We may wait a little for a home here, for all the Universe is ours—and all time and the very thoughts of God himself.[6]

MacDonald joined his wife and children at the Alex Powells' for Christmas. While very grateful for the hospitality of their brother and sister, they felt it irksome to be dependent on their generosity, and longed for a steady income and a home of their own. Things were improving a little. MacDonald had had about eight paid engagements as a visiting preacher, and had been submitting articles to the press. His first success in this line was a review of Browning's 'Christmas Eve' published in the monthly *Christian Spectator* for April 1853. He was now seeking to interest publishers in *Within and Without* and his shorter poems, but so far he was unsuccessful.

Early in 1854 the MacDonalds stayed briefly with the Scotts before moving into lodgings in Manchester. George had secured a few more preaching engagements. He went to Birkenhead to preach in February, and was taken ill with severe congestion of the lungs. He was laid up for three weeks in the house of the deacon who had expected him only for the night—a Mr Rawlins. The Rawlinses rallied to the occasion with great generosity, and invited Louisa and the babies to stay as well. Then a relative of the Scotts offered a farmhouse at Alderley for George's convalescence, and he accepted with gratitude.

As his health improved he began to look on the bright side of things; perhaps they could take the opportunity to visit Huntly. He hoped, too, that a publisher in Edinburgh would take *Within and Without*. But the doctor forbade the visit to Huntly, and *Within and Without* was rejected. The constant disappointments of these early years were of great service to MacDonald in the development of his faith. He *had* to make sense of them to himself; and his growing mystical awareness, his conviction that the world of the spirit was no less real or significant than the world of the senses, helped him to find the answer. The spiritual life was in fact the justification for all the ills he might suffer. In later life he could write,

> But what is love, what is loss, what defilement even, what are pains, and hopes, and disappointments, what sorrow, and death, and all the ills that flesh is heir to, but means to this very end, to this waking of the soul to seek the home of our being—the life eternal? Verily we must be born from above, and be good children, or become, even to our self-loving selves, a scorn, a hissing, and an endless reproach.[7]

*

When the *Christian Spectator* began to take articles and poems on a more regular basis, the MacDonalds decided they could afford a home of their own. No. 3 Camp Terrace, Lower Broughton, had been in a fashionable district of Manchester, but the district had declined, and the house was available for only £35 a year. Arthur Morley Francis, once a student with MacDonald at Highbury, came to lodge, paying 10s. a week. Angela Powell visited, and helped lay carpets and hang curtains. George and Louisa's happiness at being at last independent of friends and relations was increased when George rented a room in Renshaw Street and began preaching to a few who were eager to learn from him. This was just what he wanted. He told his father:

> Next Sunday evening I begin the realization of a long cherished wish—to have a place of my own to preach in where I should be unshackled in my teaching. This I now possess. May God be with me. No one can turn me out of this. It will be taken and the agreement signed in my name. If anyone does not like what I say he can

go away and welcome; but not all can turn me away. I call them together—not they me. A few friends contribute the rent of the place, and a box will be at the door for contributions of free will for me. We will have no odious ungodly seat-rents and distinctions between poor and rich.[8]

The summer of 1854 was a happy time. MacDonald grew a beard—something he had wanted to do since his student days. His doctor encouraged him in this defiance of fashion, saying that it would protect him from cold. The *Christian Spectator* published his story about 'The Schoolmaster' which was later reprinted in the first edition of his novel *Adela Cathcart*. A third daughter, Caroline Grace, was born on 16 September. Louisa had wished for a boy, but George wrote to his father that he liked girls best.

The Renshaw Street congregation was only ever small, consisting mainly of personal friends and more intellectually minded souls. MacDonald had hoped to interest working people as well, but they were not, on the whole, attracted to Renshaw Street. At this time MacDonald was in correspondence with his uncle, Dr MacIntosh MacKay, who was in Australia. MacDonald seriously considered emigrating; he thought he might get a more receptive hearing in the colonies. Louisa, however, could not face the prospect of a long sea voyage.

MacDonald was busy now not only with his Sunday services, but also preparing for lectures which he proposed to give in his drawing-room, beginning in September. The lectures, on English literature and physical science, were well-attended. The interest shown by women in these subjects was to lead in later years to the founding of a Ladies College in Manchester. At this early stage, with the Owens College still in its infancy, MacDonald was providing a useful service in helping to raise the standard of education in Manchester. Even the College students, boys of fourteen and fifteen, lacked many basics of English, mathematics and science. MacDonald's lectures helped to fill a vital gap.

In October he took a break from work to visit Greville Matheson in London. The two went to hear the opening address of the Working Men's College, given by F. D. Maurice. Maurice had been actively involved in the Christian Socialist Movement since its inception in 1848. Arising out of the Movement's concern to help the poor through co-operative associations had come an awareness of the working man's need for education. Maurice hoped that the College would succeed in reaching the working classes where the Established Church had failed. The Christian Socialists accused the Church of keeping religion apart from ordinary life, instead of showing how the principles of faith should inform and fulfil every aspect of living. As human problems were inseparably bound up with theological problems, so Maurice believed, theological studies should have a prominent place in the curriculum of the Working Men's College. He suggested there should be a Bible class every Sunday. MacDonald was very impressed by Maurice's approach to education, faith and work as involving the whole man. He and Maurice were later to become very close friends.

Literary success was now near at hand for MacDonald. A short story, 'The Broken Swords', was published in the October *Christian Spectator*; and early in 1855 Longman's agreed to publish *Within and Without*. Christmas had been spent with the Powells in London, and MacDonald returned alone to Manchester, leaving Louisa and the babies to enjoy a holiday with her father. Mr Powell read *Within and Without*, a copy of which MacDonald had written out for Louisa. His daughter found him on one occasion with the book in his hand and tears streaming down his face. Longman's liked the poem enough to make a generous offer for it, and MacDonald's spirits were high.

Within and Without came out in May, and George and Louisa hoped for a holiday in Huntly that summer. There were difficulties, however. They didn't want to take the children, partly because MacDonald's sister, Bella, then aged fourteen, was gravely ill with tuberculosis. They had very little money to hand, and could find no one suitable to look after the babies. Angela Powell, usually so able a helper, was at The Limes in London and would not be allowed to take charge of the Camp Terrace household in the absence of George and Louisa. She was in love with Arthur Francis, the lodger, and quite apart from the impropriety of her staying unchaperoned in the same house, Francis and Mr Powell had quarrelled. When news came in June that Bella was worse, Louisa urged George to go by himself to Huntly. He set off on 1 July, stopped overnight at Edinburgh, and continued by rail the next day. The railway from Aberdeen to Huntly had been built in 1853, and went cloe to the cottage at The Farm. He described to Louisa his homecoming:

> My sisters [Louie and Jeannie] met me at the station, and now as I sit here they are ministering to me with wild roses and wild peppermint beloved, like two fairies. They are sweet dear things. Bella and I both cried. She is so thin, I should not have known her.[9]

While MacDonald was reunited with his family, life was anything but easy for Louisa. The three little girls tired her out; teething and other childhood ailments made them fractious at night, and their mother was not getting enough sleep. She was, moreover, expecting another baby. She employed a nurse-maid, Charlotte, who seems to have been more of a liability than a help. Besides upsetting Louisa with her insolence, she ruined the perambulator, so that it had to be replaced. The new one cost 24 shillings, a sum Louisa could hardly afford, and it was very heavy with the three infants riding in it; but it was the only way they could be given the fresh air they needed.

Louisa's sister Flora, married to a Joshua Sing, invited her to bring the children to her home in Liverpool for a week or two. Louisa found it hard to summon up much enthusiasm. 'The expense will be greater than to stay here,' she wrote to George. She did go, and had a couple of weeks' rest, but in her depressed state she was unable to enjoy it. She thought she was being patronised as the poor relation; she worried about finding the train fare back to Manchester; she wanted to dismiss Charlotte, but hadn't the money to pay the wages she owed her. George wrote loving letters from Huntly, wishing she could be with him:

> My days pass so quietly—I hardly go anywhere but saunter about the house with Shakespeare in my hand or pocket. If you had been here after I wrote to you last night, you might have seen me in less

than an hour on the far horizon—the top of a hill nearly 1,000 feet high 2½ miles off. You would have seen my white mare and myself clear against the sky.... She is a dear old mare. I love her.

Dearest, my mother has got such a nice servant ... she longs for us to have [her] to take care of the children. She was three years with her and was so kind to them and good-tempered, and cares for her master's interest—a good-principled girl—and she would come with me.... I hope poor baby is better by this time, and that you have been sleeping better. I wish I could get you here.... I will stay over the wedding, which is to be in a fortnight—perhaps I will not stay longer expect you come.... You are a dear, good, sweet wife, soul and body.[10]

George hoped to make money in Huntly by preaching, but his reputation had gone before him. No doubt his unorthodoxy had been exaggerated in the report; still, the local Calvinists were suspicious of him. Some of the Huntly Congregationalists were annoyed that their minister—MacDonald's old friend Robert Troup—was to marry George MacDonald's cousin, Margaret MacDonald (this was the wedding referred to in his letter). MacDonald stayed on afterwards for another week or so, explaining to Louisa,

I *cannot* bear to force my departure. They are very sad sometimes, and I am sure I am a comfort to them ... That dear child Bella has been saving up her money for some time ... and today she gave me two sets of flannels for the winter ... Her little body will be cold before I wear them.[11]

He did preach, and got a mixed reception. One old woman thought he went too far on the loving side of God's character. Another said to his father, 'When I saw him wi' the moustaches I thocht he looked gey and rouch-like; but, or he had been speakin' lang, I jist thocht it was like Christ himsel' speakin' to me.'[12]

Louisa sent reviews of *Within and Without* as they appeared in the press. *The Globe* and *The Scotsman* were favourable, but *The Leader* was insulting, Louisa thought. She also forwarded a letter which Charles Kingsley sent in appreciation of the poem. On the whole the critics were in favour of it, but for all that it made very little profit. Louisa was nearly desperate for money. Flora bought her a first-class ticket for her return to Manchester, and there she lived 'on tick' for as long as she could. George received a couple of guineas for his preaching, and sent this, together with £3 from his father. Just before he left Huntly he was given some more:

> I have been with my father to see Alec's grave . . . He lies beside my mother and my two brothers. I thought—oh, there is room for me between him and the wall . . . My father was a good deal overcome, for it is not only the dead but the dying he has to think of. Mrs Wilson gave me £4 today 'for the children'. My father gave me £4 too to bring us home. I shall not want quite £3 and have £2 besides; so I shall come home with more by far than I could have made by staying.[13]

The new nursemaid, Elsie Gordon, travelled from Huntly with him. No doubt some of the money went to pay Charlotte's wages. Her replacement was competent and reliable—a vast improvement.

On MacDonald's return home he found other favourable reviews of *Within and Without*, together with a gratifying letter from F. D. Maurice. He passed these on to his father, adding, 'I have heard several things about my book since I returned— the principal of which is the interest Lady Byron, the widow of the poet, has taken in it. It seems to have taken a powerful hold on her.'[14]

Within and Without must have awakened Lady Byron's memories of her failed marriage. As Annabella Milbanke she had married Lord George Gordon Byron in January 1815; and she had had a legal separation from him in April of the following year. For a while the Byrons were surrounded by a cloud of rumour and scandal of the worst kind. The truth behind the separation may never be known[15], but this much at least is clear: that Annabella believed her husband was too wicked for her to live with him any longer. She never ceased to love him, and was never quite satisfied that she had done the right thing. She spent much of her energy in the ensuing years trying to justify herself. In later life—and it was at this stage that she encountered George MacDonald—she devoted herself to social works, using her immense fortune for the benefit of the poor and the oppressed.

MacDonald's dramatic poem has for its hero a great soul, Julian, Count Lamballa, who is tormented by his own genius and misunderstood by his fellows. In the account of his search for Truth, first through asceticism, then through marriage, and finally through the failure of marriage, Lady Byron had ample food for reflection on her own relationship with a man of genius. The poem would particularly encourage her to consider the question of blame and guilt. Julian's wife Lilia misunderstands him and believing she has lost his love is tempted to adultery. She does not quite give way, but believing herself unworthy and unloved, leaves her husband. The poem deals with the inner feelings of both, particularly with the question of who is to blame for the failure of the marriage. Believing that his wife is unfaithful causes Julian agonies before he concludes that he ought to forgive her; but then he gradually realises that *he* has been at fault and needs *her* forgiveness. The two are reconciled only in death.

MacDonald deals, too, with the question of a higher forgiveness. Is there a sin which God cannot forgive? MacDonald emphatically answers No. Lady Byron knew that her husband's Scottish ancestry and his Calvinist upbringing had convinced him that he was under a curse, doomed to eternal damnation. Now she was encountering a writer from a very similar background, with Gordon connections and a strong Calvinist childhood influence, who could say the opposite—that God's forgiveness is freely available to even the most hardened and wicked of sinners. Perhaps *Within and Without* raised hopes for Lady Byron that she and her husband might be reconciled and united in death.

The appearance of the poem coincided with an increase in work for MacDonald. He had more teaching and lecturing now than he could reasonably manage, and he hoped to take in one or more College students as boarders. John MacDonald was staying with them for a while. He had turned up unexpectedly, and was recovering from his perilous adventures in Russia.

Bella died on 24 August. George wrote to his stepmother:

My Dearest Mother,
Bella has only gone nearer to One who loves her more dearly and
tenderly than you do. Or if you even think that she has gone to
Alec, who has been waiting for her, it seems no such dreadful
thing. God will let him take care of her till you go . . . Bella will be
kept quite safe for you there, and you will never be separated from
her in heart. Schiller says 'Death cannot be an evil because it is
universal'. God would not let it be the law of His Universe if it were
what it looks to us.[16]

MacDonald was cheered enormously at the end of August by
the offer of a post as minister to a congregation at Bolton. A
year's trial was agreed upon; and the congregation promised
that he could preach according to his conscience. His salary
was likely to be under £100, but he would have ample time to
continue writing and lecturing. The Bolton people were
mainly weavers and mechanics, working for long hours at low
rates of pay. They wanted only Sunday services, as they had
neither time nor energy for midweek meetings. Their treatment at the hands of the mill-owners, together with the
Church's frequent upholding of that treatment, made them
suspicious of many clergymen. They may have been attracted
to MacDonald by his own poverty and by his refusal to court
the wealthy. He was never afraid of antagonising the rich. In
later life, when he was preaching to a congregation of rich
Glaswegians, he remarked, 'One may readily conclude how
poorly God thinks of riches when we see the sort of people he
sends them to!'[17]
   He preached at Bolton for two months, and a mutual confidence and love was developing between him and his congregation. Then at the beginning of November he was attacked by
bleeding from the lungs—the worst he had ever had. For days
the flow of blood continued, even when he lay quite still with
ice-bags on his chest. He was dying, and in desperation his
doctor drew blood from his arm. He hoped that the blood-flow
might be diverted and give the blood-vessels in the lung a
chance to heal. The old-fashioned remedy seemed to work, for

the blood-spitting stopped. By the end of December he was able to write a cheerful letter to his father.

The summer's financial troubles had reminded the Mac-Donalds 'to cast all on Him who careth for us'. Now they found that money was provided unlooked-for. George could write to his father,

> On New Year's Day two gentlemen called on me, who along with a third—none of them much known to me—had made up a purse of £30 for me, which they offered in the most delicate and kind way. One of the three is an Independent, another a Churchman [Anglican], and the third a Unitarian.
>
> This morning's post brought me a bank-order for £5 from Miss Ross [George's second cousin].
>
> Then this afternoon some of my Bolton people called on me, bringing me my quarter's salary in advance. They had paid me up to Christmas, just before I was taken ill. This will leave something considerable over after paying all our present debts.[18]

MacDonald also told his father of a visit he had from Count Aurelio Saffi, one of the fathers of the modern Italian state. In 1855 he was a refugee in England. He gave literary lectures at Manchester's Royal Institution, and stayed at Professor Scott's house, where MacDonald first met him. Saffi was 'much struck' with *Within and Without*, 'considering it the best expression of the religious feelings of the age. This, though himself a Roman Catholic. Indeed we soon formed a warm friendship for each other.'[19]

Louisa had been unable to do much to help her husband in his illness, as she was in the final stages of her pregnancy. Her sister Angela had come again to the rescue, and together with Mrs Scott's sisters, she had kept George comfortable. The baby was born on 20 January 1856—a boy, Greville Matheson MacDonald. Mrs Scott promptly took the invalid father to her own home, not far from Camp Terrace, and left the mother and baby to Angela's loving care. Lily, Mary and Gracie were ably looked after by Elsie Gordon.

The doctor recommended a complete rest for at least six months. The MacDonalds began George's convalescence with a visit to The Limes for Phoebe's wedding. Old Mr Powell was enthralled by his four grandchildren—the fair-haired Lily, now three and a half; the dark-haired Mary, whose parents called her Elfie; the solemn Gracie and the big brown-eyed baby Greville. He was glad to have Elfie and Gracie stay with him and Angela, when in early March George and Louisa took Lily and the baby to Kingswear in South Devon.

While at Kingswear MacDonald was seized with another haemorrhage. Louisa 'nearly killed herself racing in the dark down some thirty-odd steps'[20] to get help from the Vicarage. The doctor was fetched at once, and there followed a week of lying quietly. The attack did not prove so bad as the previous one, and the family was able to move very soon into a more commodious cottage down by the water, where MacDonald could sit in the garden and get plenty of sea air. He made a slow recovery, however; and Louisa decided they should move to Lynmouth on the north coast of Devon. They made the trip by steamer around Land's End, and stayed at Lynmouth for two months while they arranged at trip to Huntly.

They went to Huntly at the beginning of June, collecting Elfie and Gracie *en route*, and stayed for three months. It was a happy time for Louisa, as she rested and watched her girls growing strong on the porridge, eggs and cream that The Farm provided. She was delighted to meet for the first time the father and mother of whom she had heard so much, and she rejoiced in her husband's beloved hills and glens. But George was still very weak, and as the summer drew to a close it became clear that a move to a hot climate would be necessary.

5

Sunshine and shadow 1856–8

Lady Byron was on friendly terms with Professor Scott. She found out from him that the author of *Within and Without* was poor in health and pocket. Now she wrote to MacDonald suggesting that he spend the winter in Algiers; she would pay travelling expenses. MacDonald accepted her offer. He and Louisa left in the middle of October. They could not take all the children, and arranged to leave Lily with her Aunt Charlotte, and Grace and Greville at The Limes. Mary they would take with them. She seemed the most delicate of the children, the most easily upset by an English winter.

The journey south took a long time. There were hold-ups because of bad weather, and they had to stay a week at Valence, in the Rhône Valley, where George developed bronchitis. But they found themselves in a hotel in Algiers by mid-November. Mary was no trouble at all. At three years of age she was used to having a morning nap, so George and Louisa could leave her asleep in the hotel and go out sightseeing. If she woke before their return she would play happily with her toys.

MacDonald was delighted by the warmth and colour of Algiers. He admired the great variety of costumes that were to be seen in a city where Arab, Jewish, Negro and French cultures met. With his tartan plaid and Glengarry bonnet he attracted a fair amount of interest himself.

They soon found an old Moorish house on a hillside to the west of the city. They rented the ground floor; overhead was the Archdeacon of New Zealand, Edward Wix, and his family. They soon struck up a friendship. A Mr Leigh-Smith was also wintering in Algiers with his three daughters, one of whom was a close friend of George Eliot. Lady Byron knew them, and wrote asking them to call on the MacDonalds. Also in the neighbourhood were the Oliphants, cousins of the novelist Mrs Oliphant. They possessed the only large china teapot, and consequently were in demand for evening entertainments and picnics. At first MacDonald was not sure that he liked the Leigh-Smith girls. He wrote to Caroline Powell, 'They are rather fast, devil-may-care sort of girls not altogether to our taste, but very pleasant; and they seem to draw and paint well. One of them who is in poor health, is more sweet and womanly.'[1] MacDonald had never before met women like the Leigh-Smiths, well-read, cosmopolitan and free-thinking. Greville suggests

> It must have been their intellectually emancipated conversation— a little aggressive, to judge from my own intimacy with one of them—their wealth and their disregard for convention, that gave him the impression on first meeting that they were a little 'fast and devil-may-care'. They were ... cousins of Florence Nightingale, and were not unlike that lady in their decisiveness of utterance and their tendency, with all their liberality of mind, to intolerance of weaker understandings.[2]

MacDonald was able to devote plenty of time to his writing, particularly as his health continued poor and he could not take much hard exercise. He was unwell over Christmas and so could not go to midnight mass—something he wanted to do although he knew Archdeacon Wix would be extremely shocked at his attending a Roman Catholic service. MacDonald occasionally took a boyish delight in upsetting friends whose ideas of propriety were too stuffy. He hoped the shock would let in some fresh air.

In spite of the stimulus of new friends, new sights and sounds, and new ideas, the Algiers trip was not a complete success. MacDonald still suffered from bronchitis, and had more than one severe attack. Mary contracted the eye inflammation that was endemic in North Africa. To complete the list of woes, the climate did not suit Louisa; she developed a form of depression supposedly caused by the Sirocco wind. They stayed in Algiers till the end of April. By that time George had realised that life could not go on in this way. He made a conscious decision to give up being an invalid, feeling that he would rather die trying to live a normal life than go on coddling himself at other people's expense. A letter from his father may have helped him to come to this decision. George's brother Charles had got into business difficulties and had to be packed off to Australia after his father had settled his debts. George MacDonald senior, it seems, wrote to his second son in a despondent mood, for George replied,

> I feel with you in the fact that your sons have needed so much to be done for them. For me, if it please God, I shall do better by and by. If not, I hope He will let me go very soon—for if I cannot provide for my family, I would rather not add to the burden. At the same time, some of what is given to me must be regarded in a very different light from charity in the ordinary sense of the word. True, it would not be offered to me if I did not require it; but if I contribute to make life endurable or pleasant or profitable, I do not see why I should be ashamed of having that acknowledged in the way I need, any more than if I were paid for keeping a merchant's books ... You may hope that I shall not refuse to do anything that I can honestly undertake to provide for my family as soon as I return. I would far rather take a situation in a shop than be idle.[3]

MacDonald seems to have given up the idea of returning to his ministry in Bolton and Manchester. As early as the spring of 1856 he asked his father to drop 'The Rev' in his letters to him. His abortive period as a minister had had this advantage for him: it had given him a sense of vocation, helped him to be aware of people's needs, and shown him his own limitations as well as the areas where he could truly be of assistance. Leaving the ministry meant, too, that he and Louisa were very quickly rid of the unnatural strain that the ministry puts on marriage. No longer would they have to live under the eagle eye of a congregation watching for the slightest false step. In leaving the pulpit George set himself and Louisa free for a more creative and caring role than the Church could have allowed them.

A vital part of MacDonald's faith by this time was the obeying of Christ's command to 'take no thought for the morrow'. Whatever came to him, whether poverty or success, hunger or fame, came from the loving hand of his Heavenly Father. Hence it was that MacDonald scarcely ever directed his own life, but let events and the advice of Louisa and his friends direct it for him. The decisions which he himself took at crisis points in his life tended to be of a moral nature. He resigned his post at Arundel when he saw the effect he was having on the church as a whole. Now he felt that rather than live on gifts he ought to work to maintain himself and his family. He could justify taking what had so far been offered, but he must do more 'to make life endurable or pleasant or profitable'. He hoped to establish himself as a writer, and to earn his living meanwhile by teaching and lecturing. He made preparations to return to England still not knowing exactly what work he would do, but confident that something would turn up.

The MacDonalds were united with their children at the end of April 1857. It never occurred to either of them that the long separation from three of their children could be in any way harmful. Lilia and Grace, at the ages of five and two and a half, were just old enough to understand that their parents had not gone for good; but Greville was only a toddler, and he reacted badly, though he could not show it until the night of his mother's return:

> I, a cave-brute of fifteen months, refused to let her sleep. The moment she put me in my crib, I set about howling, although when she took me to her heart again I slept at once in a long-denied bliss.[4]

His childhood was henceforward blighted by a desperate sense of insecurity, coupled with the total incomprehension of his parents as to what was wrong and why.

George had produced a collection of poems during his holiday, and Longman's wanted to get them through the press by the end of June. The family stayed at The Limes for the summer, while they looked about for a permanent home. London seemed the best place; it was the centre of literary and educational activity. But another attack of bronchitis made MacDonald cautious of settling there permanently. If he expected to do any work at all it was reasonable for him to take some care of his health. The South Coast seemed the best hope, and they began to think in terms of Brighton or Hastings. A brief trip to Manchester was necessary, to settle affairs there. MacDonald saw the Bolton congregation for the last time, and said goodbye to the many friends he had made in the north-west. He also took the opportunity to visit his brother John, now teaching at a school in Warrington.

Lady Byron, now in her sixties, suffered from ill-health and was unable to meet MacDonald until the summer of 1857. In June she was well enough to invite him to visit her, and made him an offer which no doubt sprang from her wish to help him financially. MacDonald described the visit in a letter to his father:

> I have been to see Lady Byron. She is the most extraordinary person, of remarkable intellect, and a great, pure, unselfish soul. She has made a proposal to me to edit a number of letters which she has at different times received from distinguished persons ... If all goes well, and she commits the paper into my hands, I presume she will advance me a little money to work upon ... By the post preceding this I have at length sent you a copy of my new book, which I hope you will accept—both in itself, and in its dedication to yourself ... I wish I could come and see you, but I have no money, and I cannot very well leave Louisa just now [she was expecting another baby].[5]

The new book was MacDonald's first volume of *Poems*. It sought to express the deep meaning that may be found in common things and simple lives. 'A Hidden Life' is a longish poem in blank verse in which the hero, after a university education, decides to return to his country farm. The good he can do in his own community is no less because it is small and remote. The truth that is in himself and his acts will pass beyond his narrow circumstances through its own virtue. *The Scotsman* of 12 August 1857 included a favourable review of the book:

> This second volume from the pen of Mr. MacDonald is marked with the striking characteristics which distinguished his former work; the earnestness of thought, the deep religiousness, and the mingled simplicity and power of utterance are the same.... His poetry is not for the few who have erected a particular standard of taste, but for the many who are scattered, for the sheep having no shepherd. The dogmatist, if he lingers there, will find the tightly-wound coil of his prejudices unwinding he knows not how, and the

child-heart, somewhere hidden in the breast of every living man, awaken and yearn towards the truth.[6]

In spite of the lack of money and Louisa's pregnancy George did manage a brief journey to Huntly. Although he had qualms about leaving Louisa—on his return he found her very depressed—he was to be glad that he made the trip, for he never saw his father again.

He renewed his efforts to find a suitable house, and discussed his problems with Lady Byron. He was seriously considering a move to Hastings, but she thought it would not suit him. 'There is no life of mind in the place', she wrote, 'except under clerical influence; and in the matter of pupils Brighton is too fashionable a competitor.'[7] She invited MacDonald to dine with her, and asked him to tell her exactly how he stood financially. She had not gone ahead with the letters project, and may have felt that after raising MacDonald's expectations she owed him some recompense. 'I hope it is no disgrace to me to be rich as it is none to you to be poor', she said. 'If I can do anything for you, you must understand, Mr MacDonald, it is rather for the public than for yourself.'[8] She understood exactly his role as a purveyor of spiritual goods—the role he had outlined to his father. A few days later—just after the birth of the fifth child, Irene—she sent a cheque for £25, with the promise of another £50 at Christmas.

In spite of Lady Byron's doubts George decided on a house at Hastings, and in early October he and Louisa moved in. Known as Providence House, it was built on a hillside and looked smaller than it actually was. With thirteen fair-sized rooms it cannot have been so *very* small; however, George and Louisa felt that the name was too pretentious and called it Huntly Cottage. Like the Manchester house it was in an unfashionable quarter and so was available for only £35 a year. It had a large drawing-room in which MacDonald hoped to give lectures. He began another book, which he wanted to complete by Christmas. As usual, illness supervened, and the lectures and book had to be shelved.

Christmas 1857 was especially festive. Not only did George and Louisa have a home of their own, but they also had plenty of money; Lady Byron had kept her promise. Two parcels and a 'bran-tub' arrived from The Limes, and on Christmas Eve everyone was busy, from the father to the two servants (Sarah, a nurse from Devon, and Elizabeth, the 'general'), dressing the Christmas tree, making puddings or party hats or sticking Christmassy pictures on the nursery wall for the little ones. Louisa wrote an account of Christmas Day for her father's seventy-seventh birthday. She began with Mary, whose eyes had not recovered from the infection contracted in Algiers:

> Poor little Elfie's eyes are quite shut. She is very patient, and listens quietly to all the talk about the presents and the company expected ... we found our first guest, little Annie—she owns no other name, her very existence being ignored by her parents—joining our little ones in games of scampering and taking in turns to lead about the poor little blind girl.... After a short early dinner the thirteen poor children came in, with clean frocks and bright faces, to see the Christmas tree. Husband told them the story of the Ugly Duckling ...
> They all had some 1d. toy or 1d. book, or pair of warm mits from the tree ... Then they all went into another room, where they ate a cake or a bun, and husband talked to them again and told them the true story of the day—about the good Christ-child ...
> Then followed the mysterious [bran-tub] which had been the cause of much wondering anticipation all day. The poor Elf had been all the while feeling everything and getting the little gifts described to her, but never able to open her eyes ... I wish the senders of the bran-tub could have seen the faces and heard the exclamations! A history of Punch and Judy was one of the presents the tree afforded Papa, and great glee was there over the display of his elocutionary talents in giving it to the party.[9]

The family's happiness was complete when, on the 27th, Mary recovered her sight.

The MacDonalds settled down to a regular routine after Christmas. George was working on his book, and Louisa had plenty to occupy her in caring for her children. Five little ones, the eldest just six, were a handful at the best of times. The little MacDonalds were often ill, particularly Mary. Moreover George and Louisa, unlike many Victorian parents, took a genuine interest in their children, and did not expect the nursemaid to take total responsibility for them. They were unusual for their generation in that they actually took an interest in their children's toys and games, and even romped with them on occasions! Home-discipline might have been impossible for them had the family at this stage not included four amazingly well-behaved little girls. 'I do not know that my sisters were ever punished', remembered Greville. 'That girls were far above boys in goodness was always impressed upon me.'[10]

The following description by a visitor gives a vivid picture of the MacDonald home early in 1858:

> I was delightfully received by a strikingly handsome young man and a most kind lady, who made me feel at once at home. There were five children at the time, all beautifully behaved and going about the house without troubling anyone ... At a certain time in the afternoon you would, on going upstairs to the drawing-room, see on the floor several bundles—each one containing a child! On being spoken to, they said, so happily and peacefully, 'We are resting', that the intruder felt she must immediately disappear... In the evenings, when the children were all in bed, Mr MacDonald would still be writing in his study ... and Mrs MacDonald would go down and sit with her husband, when he would read to her what he had been writing; and I would hear them discussing it on their return to the drawing-room.[11]

When the book, *Phantastes*, was completed MacDonald took it up to London. As he wrote to his father,

> I had a most successful visit—got some books I much wanted at moderate cost—visited Mr. Maurice and Lady Byron—put a little MSS. [*sic*] that took me two months to write without any close work—a sort of fairy tale for grown people, into a new publisher's hands and two days after had £50 in my hands for it.[12]

The new publisher was Smith, Elder & Co., to whom F. D. Maurice had introduced him.

*

George and Louisa heard in April that John MacDonald was gravely ill with tuberculosis of the lungs. He came to Hastings, to be nursed by Louisa; but the doctor held out little hope for him. In a progress report to his father MacDonald wrote

> Our doctor says it is out of the question for John to go to Scotland in May. He must not think of doing anything for eight or ten months ... We are most happy to have this charge given to us. Louisa is only most pleased that *we* should have it to do. Though I say it as shouldn't, she is a first-rate nurse—and we both know something of the sick room ... The doctor attends him as my friend, and charges nothing.[13]

Charles returned from Sydney and stayed for a while at Huntly Cottage. He had grandiose schemes for making a fortune for himself and his friends, but they never came to anything. He hovered on the verge of poverty for the rest of his long life, and George often had to help him out. It was a joy to him to make some return for the help he had himself received. He was the better able to afford it in 1858 as he was giving lectures in English Literature in his home, and these were bringing in a moderate amount of money.

John's health deteriorated further, and his one desire was to go home to Huntly. He was able to make the trip by sea from London to Aberdeen, accompanied by Charles. He died at The Farm on 7 July.

> When the breath,
> After a hopeless pause, returned no more,
> The father fell upon his knees, and said:
> 'O God, I thank thee; it is over now!
> Through the sore time thy hand has led him well.
> Lord, let me follow soon, and be at rest.'[14]

When MacDonald penned these lines (from 'A Hidden Life') he may have been thinking of his brother Alec. He was not to know then how appropriate they would be for John and his father, for they died within two months of each other.

A few days after John's funeral his father was going out at dusk through a back gate that led onto the moor. Someone came past the gate, then turned; and Mr MacDonald saw that it was John, with his plaid over his shoulder in his usual fashion. He hurried after, but his lameness prevented him from overtaking the figure before it disappeared round a bend in the road. When he got to the corner there was nobody in sight, though the road and the moor provided no cover. Mr MacDonald was not a credulous man, but he hurried home quite awed and disturbed. He believed that his son was calling him to go with him. On 23 August he suffered a heart attack. Poulticing gave him some relief; but another attack followed the next morning and he died immediately.

George MacDonald hurried north, and was at Huntly in time for the funeral. He stayed long enough to be sure that his mother would get over the bereavement. 'For days she would pace the meadows, with bowed head, clenching and unclenching her hands held to her bosom in mute appeal against the inexorable; for few wives have such a husband as hers, few husbands such a wife as this, now left alone.'[15] She was unwilling to stay on at The Farm, and George offered to bring her and his two sisters to Huntly Cottage; but his father had left her his property, worth £1,100. She was not short of means, and felt she would rather settle in Huntly. Before coming home George went with Charles to see some of the poor people in Huntly. 'It is very pleasant', he wrote to Louisa, 'to hear how they all talk about my father. You would almost fancy he had been a kind of chief of the clan...'[16]

In his grief for the loss of his father and brother, MacDonald took little notice of a small publishing success. He may have lost interest in this particular project as it went back to his Manchester days. MacDonald had made friends with a Congregational minister from Salford, George Bubier, and the two had discussed the idea of producing a hymn-book suitable for the young. Both men felt there was a lack of such a collection. Isaac Watts's hymns for children were a great standby of the time, but MacDonald had a very low opinion of these. 'Some of them make the contrast between the misery of others and our own comforts so immediately the apparent ... ground of thankfulness', he was to write in *The Seaboard Parish*, 'that they are not fit for teaching.'[17] He gave Bubier ten hymns and John MacDonald contributed one. The collection eventually appeared in 1858 with the unwieldy title of *Hymns and Sacred Songs for Sunday School and Social Worship*.

Of more immediate importance was the publication in

October of *Phantastes: A Faerie Romance for Men and Women*. It was well received, though *The Athenaeum* complained that it was no more than 'a confusedly furnished, second-hand symbol shop'.[18] In fact *Phantastes* was a new departure: an attempt to express truths of the spirit using the fairy tale as a medium.

The story is a recapitulation in fantastic, symbolic imagery of the moral and spiritual development of man from birth to death. Anodos, the twenty-one year-old hero, spends twenty-one days in fairyland and during this time he undertakes a search for his divine ideal. The search takes him eastward, in the direction of the rising sun, which is traditionally associated with the divine. He is menaced by the ash and the alder (Ask and Embla, the first man and woman of Norse mythology) who represent human sinfulness, and discovers his Shadow, the guilty conscience that will not be banished, and which blights all he comes in contact with. He continues his search for his ideal, for his white lady whom he alternately releases from imprisonment in stone then loses. His journey leads him to the fairy palace, which represents contact with human culture and civilisation, and with institutional religion; into subterranean passages inhabited by hideous goblins—the dark places of soul and mind; and over sea. The sea symbolises the divine life, and at this point the divine life begins to manifest itself in Anodos. He is brought to a realisation of his own failures and shortcomings and finds that repentance and forgiveness are the means of dealing with his Shadow. In a place of ritual sacrifice he engages in combat with a monstrous wolf, and dies slaying it. The wolf represents the curse of mortality—the passing of time, old age and death. Anodos has become his own sacrifice, and discovers that the only way to conquer death is to suffer it. Christ said, 'he who loses his life for my sake will find it'. Having given up his lady and his life Anodos experiences the blessedness of death and a new closeness to his lady before he wakes in the real world. 'Who lives, he dies; who dies, he is alive.'[19]

By relating Anodos' adventures in a first-person narrative, MacDonald invites the reader to learn with the hero. We are to puzzle over MacDonald's book in the same way that Anodos puzzles over the books he finds in the fairy palace. What fairy-land teaches Anodos can be learned by the reader: 'Faerie' is the world of the spirit, the Kingdom of Heaven, and it is present to the world of men, to those who can read its signs:

> all the time I seemed to have a kind of double consciousness, and the story a double meaning. Sometimes it seemed only to represent a simple story of ordinary life, perhaps almost of universal life; wherein two souls, loving each other and longing to come nearer, do, after all, but behold each other as in a glass darkly.
>
> As through the hard rock go the branching silver veins, as into the solid land run the creeks and gulfs from the unresting sea; as the lights and influences of the upper world sink silently through the earth's atmosphere; so does Faerie invade the world of men, and sometimes startle the common eye with an association as of cause and effect, when between the two no connecting links can be traced.[20]

If the success of *Phantastes* was in some measure a conso-lation for MacDonald's bereavements, he was also cheered by the birth of his sixth child, Winifred Louisa, on 6 November. MacDonald passionately loved his children; he welcomed each addition to the family, whatever the inconvenience caused by another mouth to feed and another bed to be occu-pied. His son Ronald was to write much later,

> His own family of eleven children, whatever the narrowness of ac-commodation or banking-account, seemed never enough to keep the house comfortably full. During his lecturing-tour in the U.S., in 1872–3, it was widely reported that he was the father of thirteen children—a mistake proved to be due to his frequent statement that he had 'the wrong side of a dozen'.[21]

6

The literary scene 1859–67

1859 was a busy year, bringing new friends and new work. MacDonald was becoming known and respected as a lecturer in the intellectual world of London. Lady Byron introduced him to influential friends such as Russell Gurney who, at the top of the legal profession, was Recorder of London. He and his wife were at the centre of a literary circle that included F. D. Maurice and Charles Kingsley, Matthew Arnold and the Brownings. Through Barbara Leigh-Smith the MacDonalds were in touch with Mrs Reid and other advanced thinkers. Barbara was studying art at Bedford College, which Mrs Reid had founded ten years earlier. It was the first college run by women for women. The cause of women's education and women's emancipation was discussed freely in the MacDonald home. Even the little girls were influenced by it, to the extent that poor little Grenville felt quite crushed. As an adult he was to write,

> I am still crushed at times by the conviction ... that I, as a male, am still a worm. I even remember wondering how my mother could ever have married my father, he, with all his merits, being after all only a man![1]

Another friend was the Rev Charles Dodgson—Lewis Carroll—whose stammer was the means of his introduction to the MacDonalds. His doctor was friendly with the MacDonalds' doctor. Yet another friend was Alexander Munro, the sculptor. On a windy day he was visiting Huntly Cottage when MacDonald came in with his thick curling hair all blown about. Then and there Munro modelled a medallion of him, two replicas of which were later cast in bronze. Two years afterwards Munro was to take young Greville for his model for the 'boy and the dolphin' fountain in Hyde Park. Through Munro, MacDonald came to know some of the pre-Raphaelite painters—Arthur Hughes, the Rossettis and Madox Brown.

The MacDonalds made many visits to London that spring, and became better acquainted with Lady Byron. Her serenity after her troubled marriage, together with her tactful service to those who were in need of help, impressed both George and Louisa. She in her turn felt a great sense of debt to MacDonald for *Within and Without*. It is worth remarking that the Lady Byron MacDonald knew was a very different person from the vain, self-deluded, devious woman she appears to be from her correspondence relating to the infamous separation. The mature Lady Byron was deeply concerned to oppose oppression and vindictiveness, and felt great sympathy, even love, for those who were downtrodden or abused. She was not prudish, but could happily discuss details of Shelley's irregular marital life with George MacDonald, who wrote an article on the poet for the *Encyclopaedia Britannica*, and applied to her with various queries. She confided to George and Louisa the true story of her separation from her husband—something she did very rarely. George and Louisa honoured her for her reticence to the world, and kept her confidence. Even after her death they remained silent, though MacDonald did go so far as to suggest, in a poem to her memory, that she had been badly misjudged:

> *To Lady Noel Byron*
> Dead, why defend thee, who in life
>   For thy worst foe hadst died;
> Who, thy own name a word of strife,
>   Didst silent stand aside?
>
> Grand in forgiveness, what to thee
>   The big world's puny prate!
> Or thy great heart hath ceased to be
>   Or loveth still its mate![2]

He included a portrait of her in his book *The Vicar's Daughter* as the benefactress Lady Bernard, a gracious and loving woman.

Lady Byron encouraged the MacDonalds to move to

London, where George would find better opportunities for work. He agreed with her, as he was hoping to be offered a professorship at Bedford College. As far as his health was concerned he was beginning to think that London would suit him better than anywhere else. Lady Byron was considering taking a house in London as a hostel for unemployed young women, and she offered to rent it to the MacDonalds in the meanwhile. Accordingly in late September George and Louisa made preparations for the move. By October they had found someone to take over the lease of Huntly Cottage; but Lady Byron had to tell them that her plans had fallen through. The house in question had been leased over her head to someone else. This left George and Louisa in an awkward position; in some haste they took number 18 Queen Square, Bloomsbury. This was too expensive for a permanent home, but could serve as a base for further house-hunting. In any case it was only available for six months.

In October MacDonald was offered the Chair of English Literature at Bedford College; he accepted and thus became Professor MacDonald at an early stage in his career. For the first fifty years of Bedford College's existence, all teachers (except assistants) were given the title of Professor. Thirteen of the original teachers already held chairs in other colleges, and the title was naturally extended to their colleagues at Bedford. Professorship at Bedford, therefore, carried little prestige and brought in only a small amount of money. As a professor MacDonald could charge half a guinea per lecture, and could reckon on earning £30 to £40 a year. No doubt he performed some administrative duties such as organising classes, but the bulk of his work consisted of preparing and delivering lectures.

MacDonald was to continue as a professor until 1867. Mrs Reid died in 1866 leaving her money in trust to the College. The trustees, with the laudable aim of maintaining standards, invited the brilliant James Bryce to be external examiner. Any form of competition was alien to MacDonald's concept of education. He believed that a competitive spirit would be fostered by external examinations, whereas by his own assessment of his young ladies' abilities he could encourage each to achieve her personal best. He resigned his post.

Most of MacDonald's income in the years 1859 to 1863 was from lecturing and teaching, as he succeeded in publishing very little. During the summer of 1859 he was working on a play. Its basic idea was that of a father returning after many years from India, who takes service as a valet with his own son, a sculptor. MacDonald offered it to various publishers who suggested various alterations, then refused it. It only saw the light of day as a playlet under the title 'If I had a Father' in the collection of short stories *The Gifts of the Child Christ*, published in 1882.[3]

The winter passed quietly with writing and lecturing, and in the spring of 1860 the MacDonalds found a suitable house: Tudor Lodge, in Albert Street, Regent's Park. It was a pretty house, rather small for the MacDonalds, but with a large studio that was ideal as a study and lecture-room. The painter Charles Lucy had built the house for his own use, and had added the studio at the back, with a steep stairway leading down to it from the hall. The MacDonalds inherited with the house a large painting by Lucy of King Charles I bidding a last farewell to his children—a painting which the small Mac-Donalds hated being left alone with!

George's sister Louie came to London to attend Bedford College as a student. She lived at Tudor Lodge and between her studies proved a great help to Louisa in running the home. A highlight of life in Tudor Lodge for the little MacDonalds was the children's parties held in the studio. As a child, the actor Sir Johnston Forbes-Robertson had been one of the children invited, and he was to remember how George Mac-Donald

> enjoyed the children's parties [Louisa] gave in a great studio, and how he used to cover himself with a skin rug, and pretend to be a bear to the great delight of us all! Arthur Hughes used to join in with great gusto. I recall that on the walls of the studio were some casts of the Parthenon Friezes, which at a Christmas party were all lit up with small candles artfully stuck about, a most beautiful effect.[4]

MacDonald had been working on a story, 'The Portent,' which appeared as a serial in the first three issues of the *Corn-*

hill Magazine (May, June, July 1860). This was a simple love-story centring round the idea of second sight. When Louisa asked for the story's meaning, George replied, 'You may make of it what you like. If you see anything in it, take it and I am glad you have it; but I wrote it for the tale.'[5] His article on Shelley appeared in the *Encyclopaedia Britannica*'s 1860 edition; it was to be reprinted in the collection of essays, *Orts*, published in 1882.

The MacDonalds were still not quite free from the insecurity of their earlier years. *The Portent* had only brought in £40, while the lecturing fees went only a little way towards the provision of food and clothing. In October the seventh child was born—a son, Ronald—and this put a further strain on the family budget. The strain was increased when Louisa lost her purse on the omnibus; they had no money at all to feed the children. Lady Byron had died in May, and they did not know where to turn. They could only pray—and hope.

> as the evening closed in, [Louisa and George] were standing hand in hand as if waiting for some answer to their prayers. It was in the little front drawing-room of Tudor Lodge, and the rain poured down upon the weeping ash that overspread the tiny garden. The postman walked up the steps, dropped a letter in the box, and with his double knock woke them from their quietude. The letter was from Lady Byron's executors enclosing a cheque for £300, a legacy of which they had not been advised.[6]

The money was to help them through the next few years. Although MacDonald was continually writing he did not find a publisher for his next major work until 1863. George Murray Smith, head of Smith, Elder & Co., gave great encouragement, but would not back his words with financial support. He urged MacDonald to write fiction, saying, as he refused *If I had a Father*, 'Mr MacDonald, if you would but write novels, you would find all the publishers saving up to buy them of you! Nothing but fiction pays.'[7] So MacDonald began work turning the basic idea into a novel, *Seekers and Finders*.

He continued with the lectures at Tudor Lodge. In 1862 John Ruskin came to hear him, brought by his friend Mrs La Touche, who was wealthy, connected with the Irish aristocracy, and had vague artistic aspirations. Four years previously she had asked Ruskin to teach drawing to her two daughters. Ruskin grew very attached to the whole family, and particularly to the youngest daughter Rose. His lack of religious faith was, however, a source of disquiet to them, most of all to Mr La Touche, a fervent Baptist.

By this time (1862) Ruskin was becoming severely depressed over his relationship with his father, with whom he differed about attitudes to society and to religious faith. It was for this reason that Mrs La Touche introduced Ruskin to George MacDonald. She believed that MacDonald could befriend Ruskin and help him. This proved to be the case; in fact MacDonald's friendship with Ruskin was to outlast his friendship with Mrs La Touche. MacDonald was able to do a great deal for Ruskin. In 1863 Mrs La Touche wrote to him:

> I have to thank you for a great deal—most of all for what you could not help—for loving and helping and letting yourself be loved by the poor St C. [Rose's pet name for Ruskin, 'St Crumpet'.]... I don't think anyone on earth can help or understand him as well as you can.[8]

Lewis Carroll was another visitor to Tudor Lodge. He got on very well with the MacDonald children, who knew him as 'Uncle Dodgson' and always looked forward to being taken on outings by him.[9] In the summer of 1862 he brought a story he had written and illustrated himself: *Alice's Adventures Underground*. He wanted MacDonald's opinion. Louisa read the story to the children, and their enthusiasm for the tale encouraged their Uncle Dodgson to approach a publisher. Its final title was, of course, *Alice's Adventures in Wonderland*.

The family decided that a larger house was needed, and in the summer of 1862 they moved to 12 Earles Terrace, Kensington. It had the advantages of being on a well-drained, and therefore healthier, site; of being more convenient for those who attended his lectures; and of being much bigger than Tudor Lodge, though no single room could equal the studio in size. Here another son, Robert Falconer, was born on 15 July.

Like Lilia, Robert was named after one of his father's

characters. Robert Falconer first appeared in *Seekers and Finders*, which was never published, in spite of George Smith's promises. The publisher felt that the handling of the characters was over-dramatic, while the conversations considered too often of formal set speeches. In agreement with this criticism, MacDonald destroyed the manuscript. It was at a informal supper with friends in the publishing world that he got the idea for his next novel. Manby Smith, a notable journalist, told of a strange epitaph he had discovered in Scotland:

> Here lie I, Martin Elginbrodde;
> Hae mercy o' my soul, Lord God;
> As I wad do, were I Lord God,
> An' ye war Martin Elginbrodde!

MacDonald brooded on this until around it had developed a complete novel, *David Elginbrod*. He drew on his memories of home and father and set the first part of the novel in a situation very like The Farm at Huntly. In the character of David Elginbrod he cast his own father, and produced a portrait of a spiritual giant, a man whose influence for good pervades the whole world of the book. Though David Elginbrod is not the hero, MacDonald used his name as the novel's title to show the importance of the ideas expressed through him.

It is on the face of it a conventional romance: hero meets heroine, they part, hero meets another woman and only later realises he loves the heroine—a realisation which leads to a happy reunion. End of story. Within this conventional framework, however, MacDonald elaborates the theme of education, exploring its meaning and significance and raising questions about its nature, its methods and objectives. He contrasts education of the intellect with education of the soul and shows how both are necessary for full development. David Elginbrod is an uneducated man, but has a finely developed soul and an amazing power of spiritual understanding. His daughter Margaret is growing to be like him. Hugh Sutherland, the book's hero, is well educated but lacks spiritual awareness. He teaches mathematics and English literature to the Elginbrods, and receives from them in return a new awareness of the world of the spirit, but without realising his own poverty of spirit and therefore not understanding the greatness of the Elginbrods'. He has to learn through hard experience that spiritual insight alone brings a true valuation of himself and others. His spiritual state is represented by the sort of pupils he has to teach. At first, when he himself is most receptive, he has the best pupils, the Elginbrods. Then he loses interest in them, being more involved in academic achievement, and finds himself tutor to a child driven neurotic by an over-insistence on Euclid and Latin grammar. Finally, his entanglement with Euphra, a young woman lacking intellectual or spiritual insight, leads to his dismissal, and he is forced to earn a living teaching the dullest, most priggish of boys. But Margaret reappears, bringing enlightenment to Euphra, and Hugh leaves his pupils to be with the ladies. He now sees Margaret's true worth, and their union follows as a matter of course. (A happy ending for MacDonald is more than a mere reconciliation of lovers; they must be worthy of each other in the highest sense.)

MacDonald placed great importance on Nature as a channel of spiritual education, and he emphasised this in *David Elginbrod*, particularly in the first part, which deals with the education of the Elginbrods and Hugh. The seasons and the weather particularly relate to their development. Hugh's spiritual progress begins in spring, and winter brings a snowstorm that nearly kills Hugh and Margaret. It represents the spiritual death through which all must pass before reaching the higher life. A storm expresses the chaos of Hugh's thoughts and feelings at a particularly bad time, and a wood of fir-trees symbolises both intellectual knowledge—Margaret first borrows a book from Hugh in the wood—and spiritual insight: it is for Margaret a sort of church where she expects to meet an angel. She learns to see Hugh as her angel, and his final reunion with Margaret—his angel—takes place there.

MacDonald was concerned to educate his readers as well as the characters in his novel. He wanted to open their souls to the power of Nature. For the hundreds of city-dwellers who had little notion of the sublime forces at work in the world, he evoked scenes of natural beauty through some of his finest and most effective writing. Here is an example from early in the book, a description of autumn turning to winter:

> many lovely days remained, of quiet and slow decay, of yellow and red leaves, of warm noons and lovely sunsets, followed by skies— green from the west horizon to the zenith, and walked by a moon that seemed to draw up to her all the white mists from pond and river and pool, to settle again in hoar-frost, during the colder hours that precede the dawn. At length every leafless tree sparkled in the morning sun, encrusted with fading gems; and the ground was hard underfoot; and the hedges were filled with frosted spider-webs; and winter had laid the tips of his fingers on the land, soon to cover it deep with the flickering snowflakes, shaken from the folds of his outspread mantle.[10]

Smith, Elder & Co. rejected this novel too, fearing that its spiritual and idealistic elements would make it unpopular. Every other publisher had the same opinion, and *David Elginbrod* was in danger of perishing with *Seekers and Finders*, when a friend from Manchester asked if she might show it to her friend, Dinah Mulock (later Mrs Craik). Miss Mulock recommended the book to her publisher, Hurst and Blackett, telling them they were fools to refuse it. Acting on her advice they bought the copyright for £90. The book sold steadily for many years, and MacDonald had no more trouble finding a publisher.

John Ruskin was one of those who liked *David Elginbrod*. He wrote to its author,

> David E. is full of noble things and with beautiful little sentences ... It is a little too subtle in some places for a story, I think, but very beautiful everywhere ...
>
> It's all nonsense about Everybody turning good. No-one ever turns good who isn't.[11]

MacDonald was to draw more fully on his own childhood memories in his next novel. Meanwhile he continued to write short stories and prepare for his lectures. He was studying Shakespeare; his essay, 'The Art of Shakespere', first appeared in 1863 and another, 'St George's Day 1564' (celebrating Shakespeare's birthday), was published the following year. Both were to be reprinted in *Orts*. 'My Uncle Peter—A Christmas

Story' had appeared in *The Queen* in December 1861, and since then he had been working on various fairy stories. 'Tell us a Story' appeared in the *Illustrated London News* for 19 December 1863, and in February 1864 'The Bell', a story about an idiot and his obsession with a church bell, was published in *Good Words*. MacDonald now had a fine collection of short stories and he decided to gather them together in one volume. Accordingly he wove around them the story of *Adela Cathcart*, a girl suffering from a depressive illness who is cheered and cured by the recounting of stories. As well as the stories already published *Adela Cathcart* included the new stories of 'The Light Princess', 'The Shadows', 'The Cruel Painter' and 'The Castle'. The book appeared in 1864, along with the book form of *The Portent*.

The Light Princess is one of the most successful of MacDonald's stories. It is still in print today, and has been made into an animated film. It delighted readers both young and old on its first appearance. Greville MacDonald remembers that

> On rare occasions he [George MacDonald] would read to us his tales before publication, and *The Light Princess* gave me imperishable happiness. I note the fact because Ruskin, now intimate with my father, wrote condemning the tale in that, being a love story, it was unsuitable for children.[12]

Ruskin's comment here, taken with his observation that *David Elginbrod* was too subtle, suggests that he was alive to the significance of MacDonald's symbolism. For *The Light Princess*, the story of a princess whose gravity (in the dual sense of weight and seriousness) is taken away by a wicked fairy's curse, may be read as an allegory of adolescence, as a story of a young woman's coming to terms with sexuality. The weightless princess finds she can survive with some sort of equilibrium only when swimming in a lake; but the fairy uses a snake to make a hole in its bed, thus releasing the water and threatening the princess's life. The snake is a sexual symbol, as is the hole itself, which a rescuing prince has to fill with his drowning body in order to save the lake and the princess.

It is scarcely credible that MacDonald should not have been aware of the sexual significance of what he was writing. That he should have intended only this limited meaning is, however, uncharacteristic of his whole approach to the world of fairy tale and symbol. His outlook was 'Jungian' rather than 'Freudian', if such an expression can be used of one who was exploring the world of dreams and archetypal symbols before Jung was born. While one should not deny the presence of images of sexuality in MacDonald's work, it is more appropriate to his total mythopoetic vision to interpret his symbols in a cosmic frame of reference.[13] Thus *The Light Princess* may be understood to be about spiritual healing. The lake represents the divine life that can only be attained through death. This is what the princess needs, but she is satisfied with the superficial resemblance the lake gives her to earthly human life. The wicked fairy's intervention has a good effect in the end, as in all good fairy tales, for when she steals the water the princess is forced to accept the sacrifice of love. Through the prince's self-oblation she experiences death vicariously, and so is made whole.

MacDonald was no 'repressed Victorian', unable to express sexuality unless it was obscured by symbols. Sex was to him a normal, healthy part of life: his own happy relationship with Louisa testifies to something of this. And we shall see that he had no qualms about discussing Ruskin's marital problems quite frankly with him. In fact MacDonald was one of the first Victorians to give literary expressions to physical sexuality. Of course he expressed it symbolically—it was the most he could do in a culture where even 'legs' were improper, and the word 'stomach' considered coarse and vulgar (though he could and did hold up to ridicule the prudishness that insisted on calling the stomach 'the mill'![14]).

MacDonald wrote wonderfully about and for children, but his relationships with his own children, though warm and very loving, involved a certain lack of understanding. Greville, the eldest boy and fourth child, seems to have suffered from this in his childhood. The traumatic six-months' separation from his parents during his infancy made him extremely insecure. He also suffered from a partial deafness which was not properly recognised until he was a teenager. It was accompanied by headaches and made him slow at lessons. All this caused behaviour in the young Greville which his parents could only see as wilful naughtiness, and which they dealt with accordingly. As a result they had the anxiety of an apparently obstinate, shy and sulky boy. Things were made worse by Greville's position in the family as a boy between three older and two younger sisters (the other boys came all together in a group later on). George had a personal preference for girls, and his daughters were so good that Greville's 'naughtiness' stood out all the more by contrast. Add to this the interest of the whole family in women's emancipation, and a picture emerges of a small boy feeling himself isolated in a women's world, looking to his father as the only and natural ally, and receiving from him only a small measure of the reassurance he needed. Greville's summary of his boyhood relationship with his father makes sad reading, all the more because of the underlying love that lay between them:

> My father, in the education of his children, put duty before everything. In spite of his militant repudiation of Calvinism, he upheld passive obedience as essential in training the young. He would tell us we had to accept this or that on trust before we could understand it, this being the surest way to apprehending it when we were older. Yet he was wonderfully patient with me, though I was indisputably much slower than my sisters, and no sternness ever qualified his tenderness in any sickness or repentance. So far as possible, he never refused me anything I asked. I remember his saying that his own father, poor though he was, had never denied him anything, and that he hoped his own children would be able to say as much of him.
>
> I doubt if I should question his theory of education except that it made me look upon my father with some fear. He stood for the Inexorable. So that when appeal to an undeveloped moral sense failed, corporal punishment, sometimes severe, was inevitable. It compelled submission, but never made me repentant. Certainly it did not encourage my brains. But worse, it made an over-sensitive child craving for love, so truly afraid of his father that more than once I lied to him.[15]

The accounts of the disciplining of erring boys which appear in *The Seaboard Parish*, *The Vicar's Daughter* and *There and Back*, with their combination of love and severity on the part of the

86

fictional father, must have their origin in MacDonald's relationship with his son Greville.

*

In the summer of 1865 MacDonald took a much-needed holiday in Switzerland. He thought of joining A. J. Scott and his family, who were travelling up the Rhône towards Geneva; but Ruskin said that he should at all costs avoid Geneva—'now one wilderness of accursed gambling and jewellers' shops'—and urged that he go to Berne and Interlaken. So MacDonald set off with William Matheson and another friend for Antwerp in early August.

Antwerp Cathedral impressed him greatly. 'God be praised for that spire', he wrote to Louisa. 'I *would* go up, though my head ached and I seemed worn out. 616 steps, 410 feet!... I could go home contented if I didn't see an Alp...' 'I went up ill and came down well...'[16] But he did see the Alps, in spite of asthma, lumbago and toothache, and found it an unforgettable experience. 'I had seen something which raised me above my former self and made me long to rise higher yet', he was to write.[17]

On his return MacDonald applied for the vacant Chair of Rhetoric and Belles Lettres at Edinburgh University. Many of his friends thought he stood a good chance, with his established reputation as a lecturer and Scottish writer. He had to travel to Edinburgh and present his testimonials. Ruskin, Kingsley, Maurice and other eminent figures had written on his behalf. Maurice wrote:

> I have known Mr MacDonald for many years. I have been surprised, the longer I have been acquainted with him, by the extent and variety of his accomplishments. He appears to me to have as keen a delight in the literature of his own country and of other countries as any man I have ever met with; to study books as only a man does who really appreciates the authors of them; and to have a peculiar facility for communicating his thoughts to others, and for awakening in them an interest like his own...[18]

Despite the support of such illustrious men MacDonald was

not appointed. It may well be that the epitaph in *David Elgin-brod* had offended the selectors. He himself was undisturbed, confident that his heavenly Father had better things for him. Louisa was relieved; she had feared the effect on her husband's health of Edinburgh's climate. She had the toddler, Maurice, to look after (he was born in February 1864) and was expecting another baby. As usual when she was pregnant, she was very depressed. She wrote of her moods to her absent husband.

> I am simply ashamed of having talked to you with all my insane changes of mood ... why have I troubled you with them? Because I have for fifteen years and more felt as if what I felt was yours and interesting to you, especially when shut up with hideous thoughts, ugly truths and the Devil. One night God spoke to me, and Heaven came. Oh, the sweetness of that rest and that sleep in him![19]

The child was born on 28 September: another boy, Bernard Powell.

Knowing that he would be staying in London, MacDonald now took on the post of lecturer for the evening classes at King's College, London. These had been started to make higher education available to more people, and were attended mainly by clerks and people in business. One of MacDonald's students, a bank clerk named William Carey Davies, became his devoted friend; for many years he acted, in his spare time, as MacDonald's unpaid accountant and secretary.

Alec Forbes of Howglen came out in the summer of 1865. It tells of the adventures and education of a Scottish boy as he grows up in a small town, then goes to a university city to train as a doctor. MacDonald included many of his own experiences as a boy and as a student; Huntly and Aberdeen are clearly recognisable as the town and city of the book. It was immediately successful, particularly in Scotland. The characters portrayed are typical Victorian Scots. Robert Bruce, the mean shopkeeper, likes to think he is descended from the great Scottish king, but has not a spark of nobility in his whole body. Mr Cupples is a drunken librarian with the soul of a poet. These two characters embody the social and spiritual evils MacDonald is striking at in this book: hypocritical religiosity, and alcohol addiction. The hero Alec Forbes, together with Cupples, has to contend with the demon drink; the heroine Annie Anderson struggles against Bruce's mean attitudes to life and religion. The alcoholics are cured, but not the hypocrite. Mac-Donald shows his respectable middle-class readers that, contrary to what they might think, meanness and hypocrisy are worse sins than drunkenness.

Alexander Strahan was an up and coming publisher, the founder of *Good Words* and *The Sunday Magazine*. His close friendship with the MacDonalds began when he took material for *Good Words*. He published 'The Bell' in 1864, and in September 1865 he took the essay, 'On Polish'. He was to publish many of MacDonald's later books, proving a generous man to deal with. MacDonald did not, however, feel himself bound to one man or one periodical. 'Papa's Story' appeared in the Christmas edition of the *Illustrated London News*, and 'A Journey Rejourneyed'—an account of the Switzerland trip—in *The Argosy* for December 1865 and 1866. *The Argosy* also took 'The Fairy Fleet' (the first six parts of what was later to be *The Carasoyn*) in April 1866, and 'Port in a Storm' in November.

In October 1865 Strahan began the serialisation in *The Sunday Magazine* of MacDonald's novel *Annals of a Quiet Neighbourhood*, which ran for a year. It was supposed to be 'by the Vicar' and gave an account of the Vicar's developing relationship with the people of his parish, and with one young lady in particular. MacDonald drew on the pleasanter memories of his period at Arundel. Casting himself as an Anglican, he made the Nonconformist minister a godly man who was not unwilling to share the work of the Gospel with his colleague—something quite rare in real life.

Poor little Greville got into trouble over *Annals of a Quiet Neighbourhood* when he started school. His master, an Anglican clergyman, supposed that young MacDonald was a vicar's son, and was extremely put out to discover that the author of *Annals* was a Dissenting minister. However, MacDonald by this time had quite abandoned the Congregational Church, and had become a lay member of the Church of England. As early as 1860 he had begun to attend St Peter's Church, Vere Street in London, where F. D. Maurice was the incumbent. It was Maurice who reconciled him to the Anglican position;

not that MacDonald had very much against it. Even in his Arundel days he had written,

> I wish the [Anglican] Church were better. I think I should almost go into it. Don't fancy I am changing. Indeed I am not saying more than I have always said, that my great objection to it was the kind of ministers the system admitted.[20]

1867 was another productive year. The last child, George MacKay MacDonald, was born in January, *Annals* was published in book form by Hurst & Blackett, and Strahan produced *Dealings with the Fairies*. This contained five fairy stories: 'The Light Princess', 'The Giant's Heart', 'The Shadows', 'Cross Purposes' and 'The Golden Key'. The last two saw the light of day for the first time.

'The Golden Key' is one of the stories that have been reprinted in recent years. It is more of a fantasy than a fairy tale. Though much shorter than *Phantastes* or *Lilith* it has more in common with these than with tales like 'The Giant's Heart' or 'Cross Purposes'. It tells the story of a boy, Mossy, who finds a magical golden key, and wanders through an enchanted land looking for the door which the key will unlock. Prominent in the story is a wise, beautiful, old-young woman whom they call Grandmother. She prepares Mossy and his girl friend Tangle for the quest of the key, and sets them on their way. The figure of the wise woman, old but young, magical and beautiful, appears in many of MacDonald's fantasy and fairy tales. She appeared in *Phantastes*; we will meet her in *The Princess and the Goblin*, the best known of MacDonald's stories. She often represents Nature. In his novels MacDonald wrote about the work of Nature in the world and the effect it could have in ennobling and enlightening ordinary people. In his fantasies he was free to write of her soul, as she really is in her true glory in the world of the spirit. Even in the novels he could not always resist eulogising Nature as a grand old woman. In *What's Mine's Mine* he commented,

> we talk ... of the world which is but [God's] living garment, as if that were a person; and we call it *she* as if it were a woman, because so many of God's loveliest influences come to us through her. She always seems to me a beautiful old grandmother.[21]

90

Clearly, MacDonald's stern old grandmother had left him some tender memories; he associated a wealth of love and power with the concept of 'grandmother'. He paid more explicit tribute to old Isabella MacDonald in his next book, which was serialised in *The Argosy* from December 1866 to November 1867. In this book, *Robert Falconer*, he drew on memories of the old lady to portray Mrs Falconer, grandmother of his hero Robert. The house where she lives with her grandson is identical with the house in Huntly where old Mrs MacDonald lived. MacDonald also included in the book many scenes of life in London's slums, taking this opportunity to champion the cause of London's poor. Some six years earlier he had been introduced by a friend, James Greenwood, to the seamier side of London life. He had never forgotten the experience. In his biography Joseph Johnson says,

> The reading of *Robert Falconer* awakened a deep interest for work among the poor. It turned the hearts of many to the slums of London, and sent one young student to begin a ministry where the need of Christian work was great—in the East End of the mighty city.[22]

At the same time another novel was taking the lid off slum-life. *Guild Court: A London Story* was serialised from January to December 1867 in *Good Words*. The dénouement of this story of a youth disinherited by his father depends on the nice legal point as to whether the father or the sister (both drowned in a shipwreck) died first. But as with many of MacDonald's novels, the characters are more memorable than the plot. Here Poppie the street-arab stands out, together with her friend Mattie, the invalid daughter of a poor bookseller.

Some time in 1867 MacDonald was introduced to William Cowper-Temple, nephew to Lord Melbourne and stepson to Lord Palmerston. Cowper-Temple was a leading politician whose campaign against poverty and deprivation met with MacDonald's wholehearted sympathy and encouragement. Cowper-Temple's *Memorials* record the first meeting:

> A young tutor ... lay ... dying ... in our house in Curzon Street. Mr Davies came and administered the Communion to him, and

brought also to the young sick man a fellow-countryman (for he was Scotch) to read *Saul* to him. It was George MacDonald; and from that time he has been one of our dearest friends and teachers.[23]

Cowper-Temple and his wife (later Lord and Lady Mount-Temple) were to be very dear friends to the MacDonalds. George was to spend odd nights with them at Broadlands, the stately home Cowper-Temple inherited from his stepfather, and was to be present at religious conferences that were held there.

The religious life was the subject of MacDonald's next poem to be published, *The Disciple*, and of the first series of *Unspoken Sermons*. Even in the novels, his most 'realistic' literary form, MacDonald expressed the importance of the spiritual life; in the *Unspoken Sermons* he could speak to people more directly and discuss the truths of the Gospel in a philosophical, meditative manner. He could present in more formal terms themes and ideas which he had already introduced through his fictional characters.

He sent John Ruskin a copy of the *Sermons*, and received the following letter:

Dear MacDonald,
Thank you exceedingly for the book. They are the best sermons—beyond all compare—I have ever read, and if ever sermons did good, these will ... If they were but true ... But I feel so strongly that it is only the image of your own mind that you see in the sky! And you will say, 'And who made the mind?' Well, the same hand that made the adder's ear—and the tiger's heart—and they shall be satisfied when they awake—with *their* likeness? It is a precious book though—God give you grace of it.[24]

Ruskin had been very generous to MacDonald; if he heard of a publisher's rejection of a manuscript he would write to commiserate, often enclosing a monetary gift. He shared MacDonald's view of art as a means of informing and educating the public. For him the visual arts as well as literature had an important role in celebrating the beauty of nature and in revealing the spiritual truths which underlie the natural world. Yet

MacDonald went further than Ruskin, for his mystical vision saw not just the arts and nature, but every detail of life as charged with significance. The two men took a stand against the worldly materialism of their day, and both campaigned for the education of the working classes. Like MacDonald, Ruskin was on the fringe of the Christian Socialist movement, and taught in evening classes for working people. The two would argue over whether, as Ruskin held, science's inclination to see everything in logical and mechanical terms could be corrected by art, or whether, as MacDonald contended, art and science both needed faith to transcend and contain them. Both gave a high place to imagination in the perception of truth.

The MacDonalds went on holiday to Bude in Cornwall in the summer of 1867. Ruskin suggested that his pupil, Octavia Hill, should accompany them. She had first met George Mac-Donald in 1859, at one of his lectures. The Working Men's College held classes for working women, and F. D. Maurice arranged for MacDonald to give a lecture to the women who ran these. Octavia Hill had been in his audience and was introduced to him afterwards. At Bude Octavia took young Grenville in hand and coached him in Latin. Greville, now aged 11, had just started at King's Choir School. He had not had any formal education and was finding himself in great difficulties.

MacDonald held advanced views on education for his time. He was perhaps one of the first to advocate learning by discovery. In *Annals of a Quiet Neighbourhood* he wrote,

> In most modes of teaching, the beginnings are such that without the pressure of circumstances, no boy, especially after an interval ... will return to them. Such is not Nature's mode, for the beginnings with her are as pleasant as the fruition ... The knowledge a child gains of the external world is the foundation upon which all of his future philosophy is built. Every discovery he makes is fraught with pleasure—that is the secret of his progress, and the essence of my theory: that learning should, in each individual case, as in the first case, be *discovery*—bringing its own pleasure with it.[25]

Such a method naturally required plenty of time; unfortunately for Greville neither of his parents had time to spend teaching him. George would occasionally give lessons to Greville and Grace, but they were a failure, in spite of his wonderful patience. According to his theory the children should have learned Latin by reading the *Aeneid* without grammar or dictionary, but poor Greville and Gracie remained in a fog. Greville was to write ruefully,

> My father's knowledge of his children's higher needs was surer than his ideas as to how the soil for them should be prepared: he knew the awakening of their imaginative sense was, after all, more important than academic grammar.[26]

Nevertheless, George and Louisa had recognised that 'academic grammar' was essential for the boys, as they would need to earn their livings when grown up. It was in a sense fortunate for them that the girls were born earlier than the boys; they did not have to worry about such an expensive item in the family budget until Greville was approaching his eleventh birthday. Even then they had no money for schooling. However, in spite of his deafness Greville was extremely musical, a talented violin player with perfect pitch and a beautiful singing voice. He won a scholarship to King's, and his education was assured.

But not his happiness. It was a long while before he settled at King's, not only because of his ignorance when first starting, but also because of his shyness and insecurity. He was picked on by the schoolboys for little things which had their basis in his parents' attitude to life, and which he never dreamed of complaining about to his mother or father. He had long hair, for example, and distinctive oddities of dress which reflected George and Louisa's love of nonconformity and contempt for the prevailing ugliness of Victorian fashion. And then, of course, he was known to be poor, not only by his being a scholarship boy, but also by his shabby clothes. His mother once doubled the length of his misery by inadvertently giving away his new school coat, instead of his old one, to a beggar. Grenville had to wear the old coat, getting shabbier and shabbier, until the money had been saved to replace it. On top of that there was his deafness, which contributed to make him seem the slowest boy in the school.

His father, aware of his son's troubled personality, had tried to do what he could to prepare him for the world of school, but with little success:

> I think my father must have seen, before I went to school, that I lacked physical vigour, as well as mental energy. He himself at my age, though often ill, had been very athletic; and while never fond of the fearful games and school-fights common among Scots boys, he would be leader whenever tempted away from his books and the worlds which they made his own. So, before I went to school, he had arranged boxing-lessons for me, if only that I might hold my own—or as he would have put it, stand up for the right—if ever I must *not* turn the other cheek. But, because of the bad headaches they entailed, I hated the gloves.[27]

At Bude, with Octavia Hill's help, one cause of Greville's sorrow was removed. While he was falling in love with Dido and Aeneas his father was working hard. He was making improvements to *Robert Falconer*; when it was published in book form the following year it was largely rewritten. He also gathered together the experiences of this holiday in *The Seaboard Parish*, a sequel to *Annals of a Quiet Neighbourhood*. He would take an occasional break from work to join the boys dodging the waves that crashed over the sea-wall when the wind was in the south-west. He would take Maurice and Bernard, aged three and two, one under each arm and race along the sea-wall. Sometimes he would be caught by a breaker and had to wade up to his knees. It was a refreshing time for all of them.

7

Cares and concerns 1867–70

With a full household of eleven children plus servants even Earles Terrace was too small; George and Louis wished for a house that would be big enough to entertain guests as well as the family. On their return from Bude the MacDonalds moved into The Retreat, Upper Mall, Hammersmith. It was a Georgian house with a garden of nearly an acre, a huge tulip tree on the lawn and a statue of Artemis in the shrubbery. On the opposite side of the road was the River Thames with its sail-barges.

The MacDonalds loved the opportunity they now had for entertaining. Friends and relations would come for the annual Oxford and Cambridge boat race; even Tennyson came on one occasion. On Sunday evenings they kept open house. The Mathesons would come for tea and supper, bringing many of their friends. Greville remembers that

> The gatherings were often large, always happy. But no extra work was given to the servants, the family and guests together washing up the tea and supper things—'Your "Day of Wash-up", Mrs. MacDonald!' said Canon Ainger, solemnly punning, his shirt-sleeves rolled up and a teacloth in hand.[1]

Music played an important part in their social life. Grace played the piano wonderfully, and all the girls, like their mother, had sweet voices. Greville made a welcome contribution with his violin. The music was, he believed, one reason for the large numbers who came to The Retreat on these evenings.

Much of the MacDonalds' hospitality was directed towards those who were poorer. Octavia Hill owned property in

London, and once a year she brought all her tenants—from thirty to a hundred—to The Retreat for a day's outing. The MacDonalds pressed all their friends into service. There was Ruskin, the Cowper-Temples, the Mathesons, F. D. Maurice's son Edmund, Canon Ainger, the Burne-Joneses, Arthur Hughes and his family, and many more. They would bring out onto the lawn a portable stage, with scenery painted by the MacDonald boys and Edward Hughes (Arthur's nephew). The curtains were made and hung by Louisa. The tenants would have a dinner when they arrived, then go out onto the lawn to watch a play. Louisa wrote the scripts; most were fairy tales, but she also tried her hand at more ambitious works. She adapted Zola's *L'Assommoir* and Dickens's *The Haunted Man.* This last she entitled *The Tetterbys.* Tea followed, and the day ended with games and country dances. On the first occasion in 1868 Ruskin led off the final dance, a 'Sir Roger,' in grand style with Octavia Hill. Afterwards MacDonald wrote to him:

> My wife and I are troubled in our minds that in our anxiety to en-
> tertain the poor people, we neglected to make provision for our
> other guests. I believe you went home half dead with unfed fatigue.
> It was our first attempt, and we shall do better next time, I hope.
> We ought to have one room in the house provided with refresh-
> ments, but everything was sacrificed to the one end, which I hope
> was at least partially gained. But you will forgive us.[2]

The MacDonalds sometimes went into London to help Miss Hill's endeavours with the poor. She had recently become the owner of St Christopher's Place, off Wigmore Street—a place so unhealthy that several houses had been rented by an undertaker. He sub-let these, then waited for his tenants to die and thus give him his business. Drunkenness and fighting were common, particularly on Saturday nights. Octavia put a stop to all this. She found work for many of her tenants, and used the rents for repairing the property and installing better drains. The basement of one house was converted into an entertainment room, and here Octavia gathered some of the worst characters.

'Will you come and hear a friend of mine read something fine on Sunday?' she asked them one day.

97

'Parson, Miss?'
'No.'
'White choker, Miss?'
'No, he generally, wears a red tie.'
'Done! I'll come!'[3]

In tweeds and a red tie MacDonald would tell stories that awakened their interest. Only gradually did they realise that these were originally told by a man named Jesus Christ. In this way they lost their suspicion of things parsonical. Many became helpers at the entertainments. All the MacDonald family took a part, playing the piano and violin, and singing. Carol concerts at Christmas were very popular.

Although he was better off than the poor folk he and his family encountered in this way, MacDonald could not consider himself a rich man. He made more money nowadays, but it always seemed to go faster than it came in. He was not interested in being wealthy. It was people he cared about; and his sympathy lay mainly with the poor, the outcast and the neglected. He had been in London slums and knew the conditions: families crowded into decaying dwellings, in cellars or even old cattle sheds. Many more sheltered in any hole or corner they could find: in old barrels, under railway arches, in shop doorways. Without sanitation, sewers or drainage, disease was rife, and cholera a real fear.[4]

MacDonald described these conditions in novels such as *Robert Falconer*, doing what he could to shock society and involve others in the work of relieving poverty. He was suspicious of institutional do-gooding, and preferred to get people involved in establishing relationships with the poor. The concert-parties at The Retreat provided a background for friendships to be made across the division between rich and poor. They were a tribute to the genius of MacDonald and Louisa in organising something that was large in scale and yet at the same time (and this was most important to them) intensely personal.

Typically, though, MacDonald was interested more in a man's spiritual growth than in his physical environment. He saw the circumstances of poverty as a means to draw the poor man to God, thus giving him an advantage over the rich:

For the poor have more done for them, as far as outward things go, in the way of salvation than the rich, and have a beatitude all to themselves besides. For, in the making of this world as a school of salvation, the poor, as the necessary majority, have been more regarded than the rich.[5]

He faced squarely the problem of poverty and suffering in the world, while maintaining that God is thoroughly good. He was very fond of the verse from the Bible; 'God is light and in him is no darkness at all', and he often referred to God as the 'Father of Lights'. His perception of Light as a symbol of goodness, and Shadow or Darkness as representing evil, helped him to see the place of suffering in God's world. Anything that is not itself light casts a shadow when the light shines upon it. Suffering is the shadow, the visible darkness which reveals man's inner corruption. God uses it to reach out to man and help him, so that even the shadow, when seen aright, turns out to be a function of God's goodness: 'All pains, indeed, and all sorrows, all demons, yea, and all sins themselves, under the suffering care of the highest minister, are but the ministers of truth and righteousness.'[6]

This was not mere sentiment in MacDonald, but a conclusion wrought out from the depths of his own experiences of illness, poverty and bereavement. Suffering could only make sense for him if it had a divine purpose. These perceptions did not cause him to court suffering; he saw his role as a Christian to be a bringer of comfort and a reliever of poverty. But he had severe doubts as to the benefits that money itself could confer on the poor. In his experience indiscriminate charitable giving did more harm than good. And a large-scale shifting of wealth from the rich to the poor would do no good either. Enriching the poor would only impoverish their spirits in turn. Both groups have anxieties, the rich about status and possessions, the poor about material provision, but the poor are more likely to look to God for relief from their troubles. As MacDonald wrote in *Robert Falconer*,

[The social reformer] would remove anxiety by destroying its cause: God would remove it by lifting them above it, by teaching them to trust in him, and thus making them partakers of the divine nature. Poverty is a blessing when it makes a man look up.[7]

It was far more important, MacDonald believed, to treat people with love and respect—as neighbours, not as paupers. It was this that endeared him to Octavia Hill's tenants, and to the few individuals whom the MacDonalds took to live with them at The Retreat. Among these were an alcoholic and his fiancée, who came along to help in his cure. One day an Oxford graduate came to the door in rags, and was taken in. He remained at The Retreat for weeks, but when eventually MacDonald found him a post as a journalist, he left in a hurry and was never seen again. MacDonald was occasionally deceived like this, but not very often. He had a genius for finding the good in people who seemed beyond reform. In his great love for people he was willing to take risks with them. It was better to be cheated than to refuse help for fear of being cheated.

With all these demands on his purse MacDonald had to keep up his literary work. However, he was becoming recognised as one of the leading writers of the time, and his books could command more money from publishers. Although he was no longer 'Professor', in February 1868 he received the more prestigious title of Doctor of Laws from Aberdeen University, as a recognition of his 'high literary eminence as a poet and an author'. His own study was a most congenial place to work in since the artist Cottier had decorated it for him. He had crimson flock wallpaper with black fleurs-de-lis stencilled over; a dark blue ceiling with scattered stars in silver and gold, and a crescent moon in silver; and brass-ball wall-brackets and chandeliers for the gas lighting. It was a long room, with books occupying much of the wall-space. At one end the portable stage was kept. This had been in the stable until George adopted a broken-down old horse. He cared for the waifs of the animal world almost as much as for those of the human world.

In caring for waifs and strays MacDonald had no intention that his family should suffer—though we have seen that occasionally the children had to go without much-needed clothes. His intense love for his children meant that he worried about them more, and demanded more from them, than about any friends or fosterlings. Yet he did not realise that to his eldest son in particular his demands were signs of an awesome

100

parental authority, not of love. He only discovered an inkling of Greville's feelings when Louisa came to bed extremely late one night, and explained that she had had a long conversation with Greville. His conscience had been tormented by things he had done which he knew his parents would disapprove of, and he had made a tearful confession to his mother. But, she told George, what troubled Greville most was his doubt of his parents' love and forgiveness.

Greville's misdemeanours cannot have been very great in an adult's eye, but George MacDonald was never one to make light of another's promptings of conscience, particularly a child's. He knew he must show Greville that he took his confession wholly seriously, and thoroughly approved of him. He was tactful enough to make no overt reference to the intimate conversation between son and mother, but found a way to express his love for Greville in a way the boy understood.

> On the following morning [writes Greville] my father's only reference to the incident was the warmest embrace I ever remember from him ... whilst his eyes shone like stars in a rain-washed sky. Thereafter the whole world became new to me ... The transformation of my world was not, I think, wholly subjective: it came chiefly, I believe, from the discovery of my mother's and father's love for me.[8]

As his other sons were growing up MacDonald became no less demanding. He let them see, however, that his authoritarian attitudes towards them were but an aspect of his love. They had their own boyish way of coming to terms with what sometimes seemed to them parental tyranny, and referred to George and Louisa behind their backs as 'Jove' and 'Juno'.

*

MacDonald's publications for the first part of 1868 were mainly reissues of previous works. *The Bell* was reissued as *The Wow o' Rivven, or The Idiot's Home* in a special publication for the benefit of The Royal Albert Idiot Asylum in Lancaster. *The Seaboard Parish* was being serialised up to August in *The Sunday Magazine*, and then it came out in book form. October, Novem-

101

ber and December saw the publication in three parts of
England's Antiphon, a review of religious poetry from the Middle
Ages down to his own day. The book reveals MacDonald's
great depth of scholarship. He was making available to readers
poems such as the anonymous medieval lyrics that were not
easily to be obtained. It shows, too, the poems that were Mac-
Donald's favourites and which had most influence on him.
These included Spenser's *Faerie Queene*, George Herbert's
poems, and Henry Vaughan's 'Cock-crowing'. The late seven-
teenth and early eighteenth centuries—the period between
Bunyan and Wesley—MacDonald calls a 'desert'. He finds
more evidence of religious feeling in his own time, and includes
poems by Mrs Browning, Newman, Arnold and Kingsley.

At the beginning of 1869 MacDonald went on a strenuous
lecture-tour of Scotland. He spoke twenty-eight times in five
weeks, in twenty-eight different places. Not surprisingly he
had an attack of bleeding from the lungs, which he said in his
letters home was slight. Nevertheless Louisa insisted on going
to Scotland to look after him. MacDonald also suffered continually from eczema; on his way home from Scotland he stayed
in Ilkley, West Yorkshire, to try the spa treatment there. The
water did him no good, but he brought benefit to many by
giving talks in chapels and to his fellow patients at the Hydro-
pathic (the spa centre).

That summer MacDonald was invited to join a yachting
trip. He had intended to take Louisa to Switzerland, but she
insisted that he accept this invitation instead. It would be
better for his health (or so she thought), and he had always
loved the sea. The yacht was the *Blue Bell*, schooner rigged, of
120 tons, with a crew of fourteen men. It was owned by a
wealthy Glasgow merchant, John Stevenson, and was luxur-
iously furnished. Stevenson planned to sail from Largs to
Norway and back. MacDonald and three Scottish clergymen
were to be his guests.

MacDonald's eager anticipation of the trip may have been a
factor in what happened to him. It was always in moments of
stress or excitement that his tuberculosis flared up. At any
rate, even on the train journey to Largs his knee was swelling
up and causing him some pain. He ignored it for the first part

of the voyage, but at Lerwick in the Shetland Isles a doctor had to be fetched on board. He prescribed leeches and poulticing. MacDonald was unable to move his leg, so bad was the pain, and he may well have thought of his father, whose leg had been amputated for just such a tubercular condition. It was decided that the sea-trip could only do him good, and they continued on their way. They moved him into the best cabin, but he was unable to look out at the sea as it had only a skylight, so he had nothing to distract his mind from the pain. 'The other guests', writes Greville, 'all hale and jolly Scots, kind enough accord-ing to their lights, left him very much alone. My mother declared they were afraid of him, lest his horrible suffering should be a visitation for his heresies!'[9]

By the time they got to Trondheim MacDonald was very much worse. His friends saw the British Consul and got a doctor, who prescribed wine and nourishing food, and lanced the abscess which had formed on the knee. The English stea-mer *Norway* arrived in Trondheim, and MacDonald resolved to go home. They had to remove the skylight from the *Blue Bell* and hoist the sick man up from his cabin. He arrived at New-castle upon Tyne four days later, and was looked after by his host's cousin, Alex Stevenson, who lived there. Alex Stevenson took him down to London, where he was met at King's Cross Station by Louisa. She afterwards wrote to George's aunt:

And oh! dear Mrs. MacColl, I shall never forget what I saw on arriving at the platform. There was an invalid carriage and in it a man propped up with pillows looking as if he were in the last stage of consumption, with a horrid cough. I could scarcely believe it was George. His eyes were sunken, his cheeks hollow, and he was so weak that his voice, as hollow as his cheeks, could not speak three words together . . .
. . . he had suffered intensely, and who shall say those sufferings were not for other people—in what he may hereafter write. It seems to me evident enough that *this* was the only way in which he could be sent into the wilderness. He says himself that he had never had anything but the *luxury* of illness before, and it was well he should know its real misery . . . He has been getting steadily better . . . he is engaged to write a novel—a very good engagement if he can fulfil it . . . Fancy his hearing the men talk of the wonders

103

of Nature and the foreign shores, and he never saw any of them! He says tho', it was nearly worth it all—the wonderful effect of the blue sky just above him as they laid him on the floor of his cabin when they took the skylight up ... it was as if he looked out from his grave—the tall mast of the vessel rising from his cabin—that and the blue sky was all he saw—then he felt his Resurrection was come.... It was his one spot of joy.[10]

The novel that was commissioned from MacDonald may have been *At the Back of the North Wind*. Strahan had begun a quality magazine for children, *Good Words for the Young*, and asked MacDonald to contribute. *At the Back of the North Wind* ran for a year from November 1868. It is still one of the best selling of all MacDonald's books.

The story tells how the little boy Diamond encounters North Wind, a wonderful, beautiful and wild woman. She takes him on expeditions with her, in which she raises storms, frightens and even kills people. He learns, however, that for all her strength and fierceness, in spite of the ugly appearance she sometimes wears, she is in reality a good person, labouring to set right the wrongs of humankind. She helps him to visit the country behind her back—'at the back of the North Wind'—a wonderful country like the earthly paradise of poets such as Dante, James Hogg and William Morris.

The book is not a pure fantasy, for Diamond is a real child set in the real world of nineteenth-century London. His father has to earn a living as a cabman, and Diamond finds that his experiences with North Wind help him to relate to people and to find ways out of the difficulties that beset his family in hard times.

MacDonald deals here with two particular issues. First, he explores the problem of how to relate the world of the spirit to the outward appearance of everyday life. Does faith make any difference to attitudes and actions? Or what use are truth, beauty and goodness in the real world? In making Diamond an ordinary boy who succeeds in grappling with the hardships of London life, MacDonald demonstrates the practical effect for good that religious or poetic vision can have.

Secondly, he raises again the question of suffering. North Wind is another of MacDonald's Nature-figures, but this time it is a young and not altogether wise Nature. As her name suggests, she represents Nature's destructive forces and, by extension, Ruin, Bad Luck, and even Death. MacDonald presents her in her relationship with Diamond as a good, beautiful and trustworthy person, and so convinces our imagination of the good that lies behind suffering. In matters of faith and metaphysics, where the imagination leads the way, heart and mind can follow, and even children can understand. Thus MacDonald can present a very difficult issue in a story for children. To have met North Wind, to perceive that behind her all is wonderful, safe and good, is to have grasped a fundamental truth.

MacDonald's fortunes were for a few years to be intimately connected with *Good Words for the Young*. He took over the editorship at the end of 1868 at a salary of £600. Arthur Hughes worked as an illustrator for the magazine and knew something of the pressure MacDonald was working under:

> An accidental call would find MacDonald bending over his son and the Latin books, with heaps of his own work going on—the classes to visit, the lectures to get up and deliver in all weathers in spite of delicate health, the books to keep going, with monthly chapters for the magazine.[11]

The magazine did not do as well as Strahan had hoped; he thought it was because there was too much of the fairy element in it. At the end of 1869 MacDonald undertook to edit it without salary but after two years gave it up, declaring he would do no more editing at any salary. He had lost at least one friend whom he had invited to submit a story for the magazine. It had proved unsuitable and been rejected. Its author threatened legal proceedings, and told everyone that MacDonald had refused his story to make room for one of his own. MacDonald wrote to Louisa, who was away at Hastings,

> Mr. G— would have cut me yesterday in an omnibus, if I had let him. They say he thinks me just the devil. Poor man! He is always threatening his solicitor upon some one or other. I am more and more glad I am to be rid of the editing.[12]

On this occasion MacDonald had kept his temper, although it

was just such deliberate discourtesy that tried his self-control to the limit. His son Ronald wrote of him, 'His anger was fulgurous—a Highlander's; but, in my experience, rare, and never for wrong done to himself.'[13]

Some time in the late '60s F. D. Maurice wrote to MacDonald suggesting that they collaborate on a devotional book. Maurice had been thinking for some time about the sacraments of communion and baptism and

> the possibility of using them to bring men at least to some shame for their sectarian enmities, to some hope for their removal. The thought of publishing more sermons is to me rather painful and odious; yet if I could put forth a little of what I feel in some form or other it would be a relief . . . I could write some prayers and meditations upon this topic, and . . . you might give us some hymns that would cheer men's hearts and kindle their hopes . . . the prayers and hymns must both be inspirations, or they will be good for nothing.[14]

MacDonald would have found it a great joy and honour to work with 'F. D. M. the Good', as he and Louisa called him, but Maurice's illness in 1869 prevented this. He had to resign his post at St Peter's, Vere Street, in November of that year, and spent the next two and a half years, until his death in 1872, in increasing ill-health.

Maurice was nineteen years older than MacDonald, and respected by many as a theologian. He was counted a 'liberal' because he had rejected Calvinist ideas of eternal damnation. MacDonald wrote of him:

> He believes entirely that God loves, yea, *is* love; and, therefore, that hell itself must be subservient to that love, and but an embodiment of it; that the grand work of Justice is to make way for a Love which will give to every man that which is right and ten times more, even if it should be by means of awful suffering which the love of the Father will not shun, either for himself or his children.[15]

Maurice and MacDonald were in agreement on many points of doctrine, although Maurice was more politically-minded than MacDonald. MacDonald thought more in terms of the individual, and stressed the importance of his relationship with God. Both would have agreed that when all men are

Christians the state will inevitably be communist, or even cease to exist. MacDonald did not look forward to a totalitarian state but to a state where every man obeyed the law of love—a state 'wherein rather the well-being of the whole was the result of individual treatment, and not the well-being of the individual the result of the management of the whole.'[6]

Although he could not work with Maurice, MacDonald produced a devotional book of his own, a collection of meditations on *The Miracles of Our Lord*. It was published in 1870.

For most of 1870 *Ranald Bannerman's Boyhood* was being serialised in *Good Words for the Young*. This was more fully autobiographical than any book MacDonald had written so far. Ranald, like MacDonald, is brought up on a farm in a small Scottish town. His mother dies when he is young. Most of the book deals with Ranald's games and exploits with his brothers and schoolfriends: exploits such as robbing a bees' nest with the herdboy, or rescuing his little brother from the clutches of Wandering Willie, the crazy piper. MacDonald would have had similar adventures as a boy in Huntly.

By the end of 1870 the MacDonalds were realising that The Retreat did not entirely suit their health. Its nearness to the Thames was not such a good thing as they had thought; at low tide mud-banks were exposed which gave off a foul smell. Louisa, at forty-eight, was in need of change and rest. So in 1871 they leased Halloway House in the Old London Road, Hastings, and used it as a holiday home. MacDonald often stayed in Hammersmith while Louisa took one or more of the children down to Hastings. When he was working on *The Princess and the Goblin*, which was being serialised in *Good Words for the Young*, he wrote to Louisa, 'I think [it] will be the most complete thing I have done...'[17] It is certainly one of the most popular of his stories, together with its sequel, *The Princess and Curdie*.

In the former book the little Princess Irene is saved through the watchful care of her great-great-grandmother, a beautiful fairy, and by the efforts of Curdie Peterson, a young miner, from goblins who plan to carry her off and marry her to the goblin prince. MacDonald's invention of the malevolent, misshapen and ugly goblins may have had some influence on

J. R. R. Tolkien's portrayal of the evil orcs in *The Hobbit* and *The Lord of the Rings*. Tolkien knew MacDonald's two *Princess* books as well as *The Golden Key*, though he was never very happy with MacDonald's mystical symbolism. Whereas Tolkien liked to keep the various elements of his life and work entirely separate from each other, MacDonald gloried in their superimposition. To him everything had a deeper meaning, and one thing always led on to another. At a very homely level, puns and riddles were a basic exercise in the development of double vision, and even rhymes were useful for leading more deeply into the heart of things. This is why, in *The Princess and the Goblin*, the goblins hate rhymes, and Curdie is able to put them to flight by the singing of very simple spontaneous verse. They totally lack the capacity for seeing beyond outward appearances. Other characters in the story possess this supreme gift in varying degree. The great test of its possession is the ability to see the fairy grandmother. Only Princess Irene can see her as she really is, and even she cannot always find her when she wants to. When she takes Curdie to see her grandmother all he can see is 'a tub, and a heap of musty straw, and a withered apple, and a ray of sunlight coming through a hole in the middle of the roof.'[18] Only in the sequel does Curdie have his own encounter with the young Princess's great-great-grandmother.

In *The Princess and Curdie* the theme of double vision, of seeing beyond appearances to the underlying reality, is more consciously worked out. The Princess (the great-great-grandmother, who is also called Princess Irene) sends Curdie on a mission to the capital city to help the young Princess and her father the King. She is a more developed figure than in the first book, where she was to be found only in her tower room, giving advice and help. In the sequel she takes a part in the action, and appears in various guises. Again, the ability to recognise her is a test of the other characters. She is more than a fairy godmother here, more even than the spirit of Nature so beloved by MacDonald. He refers to her as 'the Mother of Light', a phrase so like his favourite title for God, 'Father of Lights', that it suggests he is visualising the Princess as a feminine aspect of God. This was a bold, imaginative step for a Victorian in a male-dominated society.

MacDonald had his own ideas about kingship and the importance of noble blood, and he expressed these in the *Princess* books. The convention of fairy-tales demands royalty for its subject, and MacDonald goes along with this. But he stresses that a true king and a true princess must behave in a special way: '. . . the truest princess is just the one who loves all her brothers and sisters best, and who is most able to do them good by being humble towards them.'[19] To be a child of God is the only true nobility, and this is shown by and in action. It is only after Curdie has proved himself in service to the King and the Princess that the old Princess reveals that he is (distantly) related to the royal family.

The snobbishness of his own society disgusted MacDonald, and he had no time for the worship of blue blood. Even his own Queen, Victoria, mattered very little to him. When she visited Ireland while he was there as a student minister, it will be remembered, he was more concerned about the lot of the Irish peasants. Kingship was important to him only as long as it went hand in hand with fatherhood; and a more telling concept to him was that of the chieftain of an old Scottish clan. The clan was an extended family, and the chief was both king and father, having a blood relationship with all his people as well as the responsibility for their well-being. The least member of the clan could claim a personal link with his chief, which gave him grounds for pride in himself and for willing service to his leader.

Willing and loving service is the hallmark of true aristocracy for MacDonald. At the final victory-meal for Curdie and his friends the old Princess Irene, in all her glory of ruby crown and royal purple, serves the assembled company. This for MacDonald is divinity. He turns the accepted notions of his society completely upside down. God is not a magnificent potentate on an elevated throne, hungry for praise and glory, but a poor man, homeless, lonely, who does what he can to love and serve those he comes in contact with. Therefore to be near God, to be like God, is not to be rich and powerful, but to be a poor servant. The place to be is at the bottom of society's ladder. The power of loving service is the power which rules the universe.

8

At home and abroad 1870–3

MacDonald's books were popular in America, but often he received no payment for American editions. This was because there was no law of copyright protecting British books in the United States, and American publishers copied the stories from books already published in England, without reference to MacDonald. To prevent such pirating of his next novel, *Wilfrid Cumbermede*, MacDonald approached *Scribner's Magazine*, New York, as well as *St Paul's Magazine*, London. The novel was serialised in both at once; there was no scope for illicit editions.

MacDonald often interrupted his narratives to make his message more explicit. *Wilfrid Cumbermede* is a happy exception, for it is written as 'an autobiographical story'. The title character comes over as an artistic creation while speaking for MacDonald himself.

Wilfrid Cumbermede and Charley Osborne become friends when they go together as boys to school in Switzerland. They share a sense of awe and wonder in the presence of the mountains, and together try to reconcile the idea of God they get from Nature with the harsh dogmas of accepted Christianity. Charley's father is a dry, severe clergyman who sees faith in terms of duty, and God as a punishing potentate. Any questioning of the Christian faith, any doubting of its tenets, is to him wilful and heinous sin. His son, open to the softer influences of Nature, would like to believe that God loves and forgives even the worst sinner. He becomes estranged from his father over this issue, and falls in love with a girl he knows his father will disapprove of. Hounded by a tormenting conscience, he commits suicide. His father interprets this as his son's last act of depraved defiance against God and himself.

110

Picture 3. John Ruskin, photographed by the well-known studio Bassano. (*Photo: Camera Press Ltd*)

Picture 4. It was North Wind. She was holding by one hand to a top branch. Her hair and her garments went floating away behind her over the tree, whose top was swaying about while the others were still. Illustration from *At the Back of the North Wind* (1871)

Picture 5. They were now, not ordinarily ugly, but either absolutely hideous, or ludicrously grotesque both in face and form. Illustration from *The Princess and the Goblin* (1872)

Unlike Charley, Wilfrid has been brought up to ask questions freely. His open questioning of the Christian faith offends Mr Osborne, who decides he has been a bad influence on Charley and is ultimately responsible for Charley's suicide. Charley's sister Mary, with whom Wilfrid is in love, understands something of her brother's misery, but cannot see Wilfrid as anything other than an evil influence. Wilfrid has to suffer while she marries, in obedience to her father's wishes, a man whom he knows to be thoroughly evil.

MacDonald's friendship with John Ruskin played an important part in the conception of this story. He knew how Ruskin's gradual loss of faith was a trouble to him, and how it upset his relationship with his father. He knew too that Ruskin was not alone in his doubts, though he had believed himself to be so. The confident Evangelicalism of the earlier part of the century was for many giving way to a period of doubt and heart-searching. Deeply religious people were asking themselves whether God could really be as vindictive as their ministers sometimes led them to suppose. If God is love, as the Bible says, what did that really mean, and could it be compatible with damning people to eternal hell-fire? Their problems were compounded by the difficulties of discussing these issues openly. Doubt was considered a serious sin, and anyone who confessed to it was a spiritual pariah. Faith was a matter of divine revelation, and corrupt human reason should not presume to try and comprehend such things. So said the orthodox. Thinking people preferred to say that reason is God's gift to man, in order that he may think about his relationship with God and so come to a more perfect understanding. This is the view that was ultimately to prevail, but in MacDonald's middle years the debate continued to give unparalleled heartache to many sincere people.

MacDonald himself had been through his own experience of doubt and torment as a student. Now he found this experience bearing fruit. He could sympathise with his friend Ruskin and through *Wilfrid Cumbermede* show him and the wider public how it was possible—and even desirable—to come through the pangs of doubt to a faith that rests on the nature of God, not on the acceptance of cold creeds.

The relationship between Wilfrid Cumbermede and Mary Osborne reflects some of the difficulties Ruskin was having in his own life. As early as 1865 Ruskin had confided to MacDonald his love for Mrs La Touche's younger daughter Rose. In 1866, when she was 18, Ruskin asked her to marry him. Rose loved him, but felt she must refuse him. Apart from the great discrepancy of age—Ruskin was 47, older even than Mrs La Touche—and the fact that his first marriage had been annulled on the grounds that Ruskin was impotent, his 'paganism' was a great distress to the family. Rose in particular had great religious sensibilities, sharing her father's fervent evangelicalism. She was torn between her desire to obey God's will and her love for Ruskin. That her parents also opposed the marriage made the decision more difficult for her, not less, for her relationship with them was also causing her problems. MacDonald and Ruskin had unwittingly caused her to disapprove of her own family lifestyle:

> As a pupil, first of Ruskin in his contempt for misused wealth, and then of George MacDonald in his teaching that God's love for man should shine in man's love for his neighbour, her home's luxury, when compared with their tenants' poverty, looked to her intolerable; and the paradox seems to have been largely responsible for frequent illnesses.[1]

Believing that parents are to be loved and respected, yet condemning her own; convinced that a Christian may only marry a fellow-Christian, yet deeply in love with an unbeliever, Rose appealed to the MacDonalds. They were anxious to help, but first MacDonald wanted to hear Ruskin's account of his former marriage. He knew that in 1848 his friend had married Euphemia Gray, and that they separated in 1854. Ruskin had not defended his wife's suit of annulment.

> My father [wrote Greville MacDonald] ... before he would be party to the courtship of Rose La Touche in opposition to her parents' approval, put certain questions concerning his early marriage; and he told me all the particulars.
> 'Was it true that you were incapable?' my father asked, point-blank. Ruskin laughed merrily and denied it unconditionally.
> 'Then why,' pursued my father, 'did you not defend yourself?'

'Do you think, if she wanted to be rid of me, I would put any obstacle in her way? I never loved Euphie, before I married her; but I hoped I might and ought to, if only for her beauty.'[2]

George and Louisa could now support Ruskin with a good conscience, but they were careful not to violate Rose's own conscience by overpersuasion. They often invited the two to meet at their own home, where they could talk informally. In 1873 Rose stayed for three days at The Retreat, and Ruskin came from Venice to see her. He said they were 'three days of heaven which he would have bought with all the rest of his life'.[3] But Rose could not bring herself to act against her religious principles and her parents' wishes. She saw Ruskin only once or twice more, then returned a letter from him unopened. She died in 1875, of a nervous illness.[4] Ruskin never recovered from her rejection of his love, though he was to live until 1900.

In the 1870s MacDonald, then between about 46 and 56 years of age, was at the peak of his career as an author. It had become a regular thing for his books to be published twice, once as a serial, then in book form. He made similar publishing arrangements in the United States. In 1871 Chatto & Windus collected all his poems and fairy tales in ten volumes under the general title of *Works of Fancy and Imagination*. Three of his stories had their first appearance here: 'The Carasoyn', 'The Gray Wolf' and 'Uncle Cornelius' Story'.

As a result of his growing popularity MacDonald received a great number of letters. Most were admiring; some were abusive. Others were from adoring young ladies who claimed that they were misunderstood; Louisa always answered these. MacDonald always wrote personally to give encouragement to young poets who wrote for advice.

In his correspondence with Richard Watson Gilder, subeditor of *Scribner's Magazine*, MacDonald discussed the idea of a lecture-tour of the States. It was a tempting thought, particularly from the financial point of view, as demands on his purse still outstripped his income. The lecture-tour would be a good way to restore his bank-balance, so long as he did not overtax himself. It was arranged with Redpath & Fall of Boston, the foremost lecture-agency in America, that he should make a tour in the winter of 1872–3. MacDonald made one condition: that he should not lecture more than five nights a week. Redpath & Fall asked for press-cuttings or testimonials, so they could judge his ability as a lecturer. MacDonald refused to vaunt himself in such a way, and was perhaps surprised when in spite of his refusal the agents agreed to his request of £30 per lecture.

Meanwhile he had to work harder than ever. As well as a lecture tour in the north of England, 1872 saw the publication of three new works—*The History of Gutta Percha Willie*, 'The Snow Fight' in *Good Words for the Young*, which was in its final year, and *The Vicar's Daughter*, the final book in the series about 'the Vicar' and his family.

The American trip almost had to be postponed when MacDonald's dearest friend Greville Ewing Matheson died in September. He had been in weak health for some time. George MacDonald and William Matheson stayed with him till the last; MacDonald would have postponed his sailing rather than leave his friend.

George and Louisa decided to take their eldest son Greville with them, and to leave the rest of the children in Lily's care. From an early age Lilia had mothered all the family, guests and servants included. Now, at nearly 21 years, she was well able to take charge. Greville pays her this tribute: 'A little stern with us perhaps in her younger days—something perhaps of her Scottish great-grandmother being in her blood— she became the tenderest, most devoted sister in our adolescence and manhood.'[5] The three MacDonalds sailed in the Cunard steamship *Malta* for Boston, and had a good crossing lasting only twelve days. In spite of unusually calm seas, Louisa stayed in her cabin the whole time.

*

The MacDonalds were met in Boston on 30 September by James T. Fields, and given typically warm American hospitality at his home in Charles Street. Louisa's letters home give a wonderful picture of New England society and the many new

friends they made. They were astonished at first—as she told
the children 'Elfie (and all Angels)'—at the enormous meals
they were expected to eat. George and Louisa were not used to
an eight o'clock breakfast which included 'fish and bird and
meat and omelets and hominy ... and potatoes and beans and
other vegetables...' They soon got used to it, however. They
needed fortifying for the gruelling tour that was ahead of them.
Even the entertainment offered them right at the start was
exhausting. Mr Fields invited Emerson and his family to lunch
with the MacDonalds, then took his guests to see Longfellow
and to admire his one-hundred-year-old house. In the evening
they went to a 'severe tea', which was a fashionable New
England expression for a slap-up tea.

> One amusing chapter in the evening [Louisa wrote to Lilia] was
> my talking to a youth, a tremendous big boy with large open eyes
> who had travelled a good deal and talked charmingly ... for so
> young and so big a fellow. I thought perhaps he was going into the
> Navy—thought he would make a jolly captain. I thought I was
> talking very kindly to him and encouraged him to speak his mind
> about things. When I heard afterwards he is *the* great preacher
> [Phillips Brooks] of the town—an episcopalian clergyman, and is
> run after tremendously, I never was more flabbergasted.[6]

Phillips Brooks (author of the Christmas carol 'O Little Town
of Bethlehem') was later to say of MacDonald's preaching,

> As I listened, I seemed to see how weak in contrast was the way in
> which other preachers had amused me and challenged my admir-
> ation for the working of their minds. Here was a gospel. Here were
> real tidings. And you listened and forgot the preacher.[7]

MacDonald's first lecture, in the Union Hall at Cambridge-
port, was on 'Robert Burns', a subject he had not tackled
before. He gave a second on the Scottish poet to an audience of
over 2,800 at the Lyceum in Boston itself. He always lectured
without notes, using only a small copy of the text he was
discussing, in this case a volume of Burns's poems. Greville attended the lecture. He says,

> he set the man before them, the lover, the romantic ploughman,
> the poet, in true portraiture, while his sins and shortcomings were

fully accredited to him. I must have heard him lecture on Burns over forty times, I think, in the States, and . . . on every occasion it was a different lecture.[8]

He got a rapturous reception. Mr Fields shook him by the hand with tears in his eyes, saying there had been nothing like it since Dickens. Then Mr Redpath rushed up: 'See here, Mr MacDonald, why didn't you *say* you could do this sort of thing? We'd have got over 300 dollars a lecture for you! Guess the Lyceums all over the United States'll think they've *done* Redpath and Fall, sure! You make me sick! Yes, *Sir.*'

MacDonald went at the end of October to Amesbury, to lecture and to visit Whittier, the Quaker poet. A girl who was present at that meeting said the four-line 'Baby Sermon' from *At the Back of the North Wind* seemed particularly appropriate to MacDonald himself:

> The lightning and thunder,
>   They go and they come;
> But the stars and the stillness
>   Are always at home.[9]

After a visit to Providence, Rhode Island, MacDonald returned to the Boston Lyceum, lecturing on Tom Hood (famous for 'The Song of the Shirt'). There followed a brief visit to New York, where the MacDonalds met J. G. Holland, editor of *Scribner's Magazine*, and his family. Then they travelled to Philadelphia, where they were entertained in great splendour by the Lippincotts. MacDonald lectured in the Opera House to a full audience of 3,500. From Philadelphia via Scotch Plains, New Jersey, they came to Washington. Mr and Mrs Gurney were their hosts here. Russell Gurney had recently been appointed British representative on the Commission to settle British and American claims arising out of the Civil War of 1861–5. The Gurneys gave a reception for MacDonald and for Professor Tyndall, the physicist, who was also lecturing in Washington.

A charming *débutante* being introduced to my father [records Greville] began telling him how much she had profited by his teaching. Some of his words on *Light* she'd never forget... 'But', she

118

rattled on, 'your great work on *The Glaciers of the Alps*, well, I've *studied* that . . .'[10]

At this point, according to the gossip columnist of *The Capital*, MacDonald, who had been staring 'like a featherless owl', 'colored up to the hair and fled the encounter in such confusion that the company feared he was suffering from a relapse of his late sickness'.[11] But Greville, who was there, gives a different ending:

> But here Mrs Russell Gurney, with her quiet tact, came to my father's rescue, and the sweet impostor was led away by one of the private secretaries, perhaps to be presented to the most militant atheist of the day and to thank him for *Robert Falconer*.[12]

On 25 November the Gurneys put the MacDonalds on a train for a visit to Baltimore. On her return Mrs Gurney wrote to Lilia,

> This morning we have seen them off in a little compartment all to themselves in one of the huge cars . . . How many he has met with who feel they owe him unspeakable things! It seemed to me that I was seeing him reaping in joy and bringing his sheaves with him, after the sowing in tears of past years.[13]

She soon had George and Louisa back with her. This time George was struck down with a severe attack of bronchitis and, to Redpath's annoyance, Louisa cancelled several of his lectures. The position was quite serious, as she said in a letter to Lilia:

> I never saw him more prostrate, except, of course, at the time of the Manchester illness. It is very serious this attack for him—we do not know yet whether he will be able to lecture again at all, and if he does he can scarcely make up all he has lost before the close of the lecture season . . . We have given up Chicago. I wrote letters enough yesterday to put off lectures this side of Christmas to the value of over £300. Was it not trying for him? But he is so good—he lets me do just as I like and I write away to everybody.[14]

But MacDonald had a wonderful resilience, due in part to the optimism generated by his faith, and in part to his gift of being able to fall asleep anywhere, at any time. He must have had a very relaxed frame. So he recovered quickly, and was soon able to go out driving with Louisa, to the indignation of the doctor. They travelled by Pullman car to Elmira, New York, where they stayed with Samuel Clemens (Mark Twain) and his family. 'We are revelling in *lapsury's luck*', wrote George to Lilia. He and Clemens got on very well together. Their approach to religion was in many ways similar, and they discussed the possibility of their co-operating in the writing of a novel. The project was never begun, however.

The MacDonalds went at Christmas to the Gilders' home at Newark, New Jersey, and enjoyed a well-earned rest. MacDonald was able to send home £400 in the new year, most of which went to pay debts. The Gilders delighted in entertaining the MacDonalds. Richard thought of them as an extra father and mother, and of himself as the twelfth child. He wrote to Lilia:

> Does it seem possible to you that a three-thousand-miles-away man-boy—whom you have never seen—should delight in such little services to [George MacDonald] *almost* as much as you? Can you imagine that he feels as if he knew the whole ten at home, individually—and is as much interested in hearing about ... the making of Christmas presents—as the three wanderers are?
>
> You might imagine that; but you can never know how the hearts of unknown multitudes are uplifted by the words that fall from the father's lips—you can never now how many here look upon him as a father indeed.[15]

But Louisa and George wanted a little independence and, at the risk of offending, Louisa refused many offers of hospitality in favour of lodgings in New York for two weeks. They lived a delightfully bohemian life, with impromptu lunches fetched from the pastrycook's or the ice cream store. Many young people came to visit them, among them such independent ladies as Helena De Kay (who married Richard Gilder) and Maria Oakey; they shared a studio in Broadway, and painted Greville's portrait.

One lecture was to be given at Princetown, New Jersey—a three-hours' journey. Louisa described the visit to Lily:

> [We stayed] at a Scotch Presbyterian minister's house ... very

pleasant people, a beautiful white-headed man, with a very nice wife and some sweet Scotch lassie daughters. . . . Papa gave such a glorious lecture on *Macbeth*. He is improving so wonderfully in dramatic power. It's lovely. He really sent us all into the cold shivers last night over the Ghost scene and the sleep walking scenes! He gets so eager and strong on what he has to say that it pours out with great flashes of eloquence that astonish even me. All the divines and the young men, 500 students, listened to him last night. Imagine *Macbeth* in a Presbyterian Church! This is quite the hot bed of the old Theology too, and yet they came out to hear him! And this old Dr. McCosh *asked Papa to preach!*[16]

They went twice to hear the choir of emancipated slaves, the Jubilee Singers, while in New York—they were so impressed with their performance. They talked to them afterwards and urged them to visit England. During the conversation the gas lights were suddenly turned off. 'All one colour now!' one of the singers shouted out. The Jubilee Singers followed the Mac-Donalds' advice and made a highly successful tour of England in 1874.

As early as February 1871 MacDonald had received an invitation from the Burns Society of New York to be their guest at the Burns Night dinner. He had asked, in accepting, whether the American Scots followed the custom of appearing in full national dress. The reply came that it was *de rigueur* for Highlanders to wear the kilt. Accordingly MacDonald went on 24 January in his MacDonald tartans, complete with sword, dirk and *skian dubh*. He found everyone else in black swallow-tails and white tie; they received him with rapturous applause! As the guest of the evening he responded to the toast, 'Scottish Literature', and took the opportunity to explain his dress and to threaten vengeance on the particular friend who had deliberately misled him!

At the end of January the touring began again. It was in the middle of the New England winter and the weather was severe. A short stay at Elmira brought no problems, but from there they had to get to Pittsburgh. They intended to make the journey in easy stages, but did not imagine it would take them all of four days. Their train was twice held up by derailments on the line ahead of them, and the only way they could keep their

appointment in Pittsburgh was to abandon their luggage—
which included George's lecture books and his greatcoat—at
Harrisburg, and take a sleeping car. Even then the last leg of
the journey took seventeen hours instead of the scheduled
eleven. It was the coldest night of the winter, and George
nearly died. The conductor let them warm themselves at the
stove in his own compartment, and so the lecturer was saved.
At Pittsburgh he had to lecture on 'Macbeth' instead of 'Tom
Hood' as he had intended, owing to the temporary loss of his
lecture books. The *Methodist Recorder* of 8 Feb. 1873 gives this
account of the lecture:

> He sketched in a masterly manner the fearful progress [Macbeth
> and his wife] both made in evil, when once they had yielded to
> temptation. Such topics as the sinfulness of ambition, the wrongs a
> man may do to his conscience, the fearful progress in moral de-
> terioration which is made by men or women when they first follow
> their inclinations without self-restraint, were handled with a thrill-
> ing power ... [George MacDonald] is natural, easy and genial,
> without any pet-phrases or kill-time mannerism. One feels in com-
> pany with a hearty friend, in sitting near MacDonald, seeing his
> manly face and hearing his honest brogue... We were shown a
> photograph of the whole family—a sunny-faced and radiant
> group, with little Maurice among them, the lad who suggested, his
> mother said, by his quaint sayings, that weird writing, 'On the
> back of the North Wind'.[17]

In February they journeyed to Cincinnati, where MacDonald
had second cousins, the Spences. They were warmly entertained, first by Dr Spence and then by his brother James, both
of whom were tobacco manufacturers. James's two little girls
were the only quiet children Louisa had seen in the States, and
the black 'Mammy' was the only happy servant she had seen.
The lectures did not go so well in Cincinnati. 'But what could
we expect', writes Greville, 'when the population was chiefly
pigs, and even driving a buggy through the snorting throngs
that filled roadway and side-walks everywhere, scarcely
roused them? Cincinnati was then known as Porkopolis.'[18]
It was decided to extend the tour to make up for the cancelled lectures. Some local agencies refused the full fee for these
new lectures, claiming MacDonald had broken his contract.

Louisa was suffering from severe headaches and fatigue, while George's health seemed, on the whole, to improve. They found some rest at Milton, Massachusetts, where, on 8 March, their twenty-second wedding anniversary, they received this letter from Richard Gilder:

Dear Mommy and Papa,
   Here's your good health, and your family—and may they all live long and prosper! including the twelfth infant. We all drank to you at Dr Holland's this wedding-day morning amid the clink of goblets (of water) and crinkle of buckwheat cakes.
   I've curdled and groaned and wept over *The Haunted House*; and now we shall see what effect it has upon the printer.
            'Outside, forsaken, in the dim
            Phantom-haunted chaos grim
            He stands with the deed going on in him!'
is the stunningest thing I can think of. It twists one's heart up into hard knots and sends the blood into one's boots with a bound. G. MacD. has almost outdone himself this time! . . . I am very fond of you, so are a great many thousand other people—but not so much.
            For ever and a day thine,
            R. Watson Gilder, alias the Boy Dick.[19]

The poem was duly published in *Scribner's Magazine*. It contained the novel and striking idea that the haunted house did not simply contain a ghost; it was itself the ghost. It was inspired by a work of Thomas Moran, famous for his pictures of the Yellowstone country.
   Back at Boston, they saw a performance of *Macbeth* that gave George and Louisa an idea. George wrote to Lily,

Seriously I am inclined to try how it feels to be a murderer. I find I can learn Macbeth's part very easily for me, and before we come home expect to be complete in it, as far as the words go. Whether I can act it is another thing, but if you will be Lady Macbeth I will try. What made me think of it, and Mamma too, was seeing the latter done pretty well and the former very ludicrously the other night . . .[20]

After another brief visit to New York they set out for Chicago, via Niagara. They were scheduled to call at Buffalo, then Hamilton and Toronto in Canada before stopping at Ann

Arbor, and Chicago. At Chicago MacDonald gave his fortieth lecture on 'Robert Burns'. A high point of the tour was an extra visit to Ann Arbor on their return from Chicago. They stayed at the home of the Rev Mr Fisk, son-in-law to old Mrs Spence, first cousin to MacDonald's father, and mother to the Cincinnati relatives. The old lady spent a delightful time with George, talking about old times in and around Huntly. This reminder of his home, his father and his grandmother drew out the best from him when he preached on the Sunday, as Louisa wrote to Lily:

> Father has been preaching so divinely, so simply, so powerfully. All the other places in the town, except the Episcopalians, shut their churches that their ministers and their congregations might have the opportunity of hearing him . . . if ever he was speaking the truth as if by the power of the Spirit within him, it was tonight. I hung on every word as an utterance from the voice of the Father speaking through him . . . The effect was tremendous, the listening was silence itself. He was so overcome afterwards that I was afraid for him—and he has to lecture to-morrow.[21]

Since the early 1860s MacDonald had taken no money for preaching. In the States it annoyed Mr Redpath that people should be able to hear 'his' lecturer free of charge. He may have feared attendances at the lectures would be lower, although if anything the numbers were increased.

The tour was now coming to an end, with a few lectures in Massachusetts and Vermont, and a final visit to Boston. At a farewell dinner party there MacDonald's Boston friends presented him with a 'Copyright Testimonial' of over $1500, in recognition of the fact that many of his books in America had brought him no money at all. The last few days in the States were spent with the Hollands in New York. There the deacons of a Fifth Avenue church came to ask if he would accept its pastorate at a salary of $20,000 (worth about £150,000 today). He refused at once, perhaps sickened by their assumption that a fellow-Christian could morally accept such a staggering sum in a country where poverty was widespread. He was already doing the work God had given him, and that was reward enough for him.

His friends asked him to give a farewell lecture on 'Hamlet' in the Association Hall, for which MacDonald was to receive all the takings. The place was packed. After the lecture Dr Henry Bellows gave the farewell greetings of those present. MacDonald replied with these words:

> We came loving you, and knowing that we should love you yet more; and instead of being disappointed our hearts are larger and fuller for the love of so many more friends than we had before.... And as you and I, whate'er befall, will never find misunderstanding possible, so may it be with our fellow countrymen, yours and mine. Never let us misunderstand each other, whatever we do. Let there be no lies between us.... I trust and hope that we in England and you in America, who have the same blood, and the same language, and the same literature, the same Shakespeare, not to speak of the same Bible, will only be the better friends for everything that compels us to explain what we mean to each other.[22]

So they sailed for Southampton in May. The tour had been a great success, for though MacDonald had not earned more than £1000 he had won acclaim from the public at large, and he and Louisa had made many friends. Richard Gilder wrote to Lily that her mother had 'carried all hearts by storm ... We expected that of the father—but the mother took America by surprise, you see.'[23]

More than anything else the tour had laid the foundation of a good relationship between George MacDonald and his eldest son. For perhaps the first time Greville was encountering MacDonald not as a parent but as a public figure, a lecturer and preacher. It made a world of difference; he saw his father with new eyes.

> In taking me with them to America [wrote Greville], my parents opened the house-door for me, and gave me its latch-key. Closer companionship let me understand better their courage and devotion, as well as my father's bold facing of his day's militant materialism; how he was strengthened by his intense love for men, women and children, and by faith in that beauty ... in which their Creator found for them delight and believing. I began to see how indeed it was my father's passion for God, rather than his logical intellect or his superb eloquence, that made men follow him.[24]

Henceforward father and son were to grow closer to each other. Problems and difficulties lay ahead, but in their overcoming MacDonald came to cherish a special regard for his firstborn son, and to feel that of all his children, Greville understood him best. Reflecting many years later on the American trip and his father's success as a lecturer, Greville could see how George MacDonald himself unconsciously embodied his own ideal of royal and divine service, expressed in personal relationships:

> It was the personal appeal by which he always kept his audience spellbound, and sent them away, not only with thoughts that would never wither, but with hope to search for the heritage that is every man's for the finding. One may well claim that the personal touch is always royal, a spiritual giving away; and that, while it heals, it compels the poorest in heart to go and do likewise.[25]

9

The shadow of death: 1873–84

MacDonald came back to England with renewed mental vigour. He got to work at once on *Malcolm*, a story about a fisher-lad who turns out to be a nobleman. He had already, in the summer of 1872, made a trip to Scotland for background detail. He managed to get through an amazing amount of work in the next few years, in spite of recurring illness. At the same time as *Malcolm*, he was working on *St George and St Michael* and *A Double Story*; then came *Thomas Wingfold, Curate*, an essay on Shakespeare ('The Elder Hamlet'), and a book of translations of German and Italian poetry entitled *Exotics*. This period also saw the development of his ideas about 'divine service' in *The Marquis of Lossie*, the sequel to *Malcolm*. In the later work Malcolm, legally but not socially recognised as a Scottish Marquis, is content to serve as his half-sister's groom so that he can enjoy her confidence and encourage her to do right. Only when she falls under the influence of the idle and profligate London aristocracy does Malcolm take the power that is rightfully his. *The Princess and Curdie*, which was discussed in the previous chapter, was written shortly after *The Marquis of Lossie*. MacDonald frequently presented his ideas in more than one literary form. The novels explore in real and contemporary terms the working-out of themes presented timelessly in fantasy, fairy tale or poetry.

He was conscious that his urgent need to communicate important truths about the nature of God and the way he works in both natural and supernatural worlds, could have a deleterious effect on his writing from an artistic point of view. His preaching of his Gospel, his constant emphasis on his message, meant that his novels were marred as literature. Yet it was—and still is—this very quality that endeared him to many readers. His aphorisms and images of the spiritual life helped them to a new understanding of their faith and of themselves. His son Ronald wrote:

> Once I asked him why he did not, for change and variety, write a story of mere human passion and artistic plot. He replied that he would like to write it. I asked him further whether his highest literary quality was not in a measure injured by what must seem to many the monotony of his theme—referring to the novels alone. He admitted that it was possible; and went on to tell me that, having begun to do his work as a congregational minister, and having been driven ... into giving up the professional pulpit, he was no less impelled than compelled to use unceasingly the new platform whence he had found that his voice could carry so far.[1]

For the sake of his readers MacDonald sacrificed his literary reputation and was content to be remembered as a second-rate novelist.

Edward Hughes, Arthur's nephew, had been a close friend of the MacDonalds for some years, and a particular admirer of their daughter Mary. He proposed to her in the autumn of 1873. The engagement was a cause of great family rejoicing, but it did not lead to marriage. In 1874 Mary contracted scarlet fever. She recovered from this, but tuberculosis began to affect her lungs. She had been the strongest of the family— Wilfred Dodgson (Lewis Carroll's brother) had taught her to box—but now she lost weight rapidly. Hopes for her marriage had to be put off.

Both George and Louisa wanted to leave The Retreat, believing that its site was the cause of Mary's illness. In the spring of 1875 they took the old farmhouse of Great Tangley Manor, near Guildford, for six months. Its antiquity was a great delight to George; it was built in 1582. The younger boys were installed there with a tutor. George and Louisa, aware of their failure to provide young Greville with a grounding in Latin and mathematics, had found an excellent young man to take charge of Robert, Maurice, Bernard and MacKay. Greville was by now a medical student. Ronald may have been away at boarding school. MacDonald could ride between Hammersmith and Great Tangley, for he now had a horse,

bought for him by Louisa out of the small income she had inherited from her father. He had died in 1870, aged 90. Relatives thought the horse an unwarranted luxury; Louisa's
brother-in-law Joshua Sing visited specially to grumble, but
George's own opinion was, as the proverb says, 'there is nothing so good for the inside of a man as the outside of a horse.'
When Joshua got home he sent a cheque to pay for the mare's
first year's keep.

A return to The Retreat for the following winter was out of
the question. Halloway House was no longer available to
them, so they turned to Bournemouth, which had a good reputation for the cure of tuberculosis. They took a newly-built
house at Boscombe and named it 'Corage', the first word in
MacDonald's motto, 'Corage! God mend al!'—an anagram of
'George MacDonald'. Henry Cecil, an old friend from Manchester, had moved to a house nearby, for the sake of his wife.
When she died, soon afterwards, Cecil gave her two Shetland
ponies and their carriage to Louisa. Louisa used to drive them
herself, though she always said she had no control over them.
However that may be, the ponies always delivered her safely
wherever she wished to go. MacDonald included them in what
is in some ways his best novel, *Paul Faber, Surgeon*. There they
figure as Zephyr and Zoe: 'They were the tiniest, daintiest
things, of the smallest ever seen in harness, but with all the
ways of big horses, therefore amusing in their very grace. They
were the delight of the children of ... the villages round.'[2]

Before *Paul Faber, Surgeon* comes *Thomas Wingfold, Curate*.
This was published in book form in 1876 and also serialised in
Strahan's new periodical, *Day of Rest*. Thomas Wingfold represents the ideal clergyman, and was one of MacDonald's
favourite characters. He appears also in *Paul Faber, Surgeon* and
in *There and Back*. *Thomas Wingfold, Curate* tells the story of the
curate's conversion to true Christianity. He is challenged by a
man of the world, 'Do you honestly believe all the humbug you
preach?' The honest Thomas has to admit that he does not,
and thus begins his spiritual development.

MacDonald's love for friends and enemies was well known
in his immediate circle. Ronald MacDonald believed he could
go further. He wrote that equally, 'in the proper circumstance

of human strife, he could have killed his friend without a stain of conscience.'[3] For MacDonald the conscience was all-important; individual wrong lay in acting against one's conscience. Hence, although he was a pacifist, he could imagine and approve a soldier fighting for a cause he believed in. He wrote about such a situation in *St George and St Michael*, his only historical novel. The two saints represent opposing sides in the Civil War, in which friends and brothers were to be found fighting against each other.

*

From the early days at The Retreat, the whole family had taken a delight in amateur dramatics. George's latent acting ability had been developed by his American tour and, as we have seen, he decided to learn the part of Macbeth. Lilia and Bernard were the best actors; in fact Bernard was to become Professor of Elocution at King's College.[4] Lilia had known Shakespeare's plays from the age of eleven. Kate Terry, Phelps, and Forbes-Robertson, who were the foremost actors of the day, agreed that Lilia had wonderful abilities. Phelps hoped to play Macbeth to her Lady Macbeth on the London stage, but it was not to be. The moral tone of the acting world was so low, and the temptations for a young girl so great, that George and Louisa could not consent to let her pursue an acting career.

However, the family theatricals continued and eventually became semi-professional. At Hastings the MacDonalds had met a Miss Kingsbury who ran a convalescent home. To raise money for this home, Louisa organised a public performance of *The Tetterbys*. The more sedate of their friends and relations protested, but to no avail. The production was a great success and Louisa decided to present more plays, this time to help the family finances. She dramatised the second part of *The Pilgrim's Progress*, casting Lilia as Christiana and her husband as Mr Greatheart. George and Louisa's twenty-sixth wedding anniversary, 8 March 1877, saw the first public performance given at Christchurch, Hampshire. Local press reviews praised the performance and waxed enthusiastic about Lilia's gifts.

Greville was uneasy in his own mind about the acting business. His younger brothers' studies were being interrupted, and he hated the idea of his mother and sisters making a display of themselves:

> It never distressed me to see my eldest sister play in public—and precisely because her own person vanished in her art; whereas the fact that the others could not conceal their identity made it inexpressibly painful. I told my father all I felt, and I do not forget his sympathy with me—nor the admission that himself had felt much as I did, but that, my mother being so sure this work was given her to do, he must bow to her interpretation of God's will . . . He took it as a humbling of his worldly pride; and he would have me realise better my mother's singleness of heart, her devotion to her darlings' interests.[5]

As this implies, MacDonald tended to idolise Louisa; in fact he habitually gave way to her. Very rarely would he take a conscious decision to direct his own life. He took things very much as they came. His frequent illnesses helped him to defer to his wife, for they both accepted that she was responsible for him as his nurse. This might well mean, as for example it frequently did in the USA, that engagements had to be cancelled, on Louisa's insistence. This overruling on her part probably made her feel guilty about standing in the way of her husband's career, and led indirectly to her persisting in the acting. She saw it as a sort of recompense to him and a way she could make up for the money lost through her interference.

But now MacDonald's burst of activity had worn him out. He was suffering more frequent illness, which meant that he had to work even harder when he was well. His usual plan was to sketch out a whole book for his publisher, who would then publish each of three parts as MacDonald completed them. If he was pressed for time he would have to begin the first part without submitting a sketch. There would be problems if the publisher found he did not like the work, say, in the middle of part two. On one occasion, Greville MacDonald records,

> the publisher was dissatisfied, and the author, rather than modify his methods or have any dispute, refunded the £100 paid him in advance, though he had to borrow it, at 5 per cent. and did it in

spite of his agent, Mr A. P. Watt's protests. Nor would he accept a refunding of the latter's commission.[6]

George and Louisa were increasingly worried about Mary's health. In the autumn of 1877 they decided that she should go to Italy rather than face another English winter. Louisa took Lily, Mary, Irene and Ronald. They stayed at Mentone on the Riviera and at Genoa, before settling at Nervi. There they took the Palazzo Cattaneo (described by Greville as a 'great bare house, with its shabby mural paintings and quiet oratory'[7]) for the winter. MacDonald hoped to join them, but various things kept him in England. For a time he tried to work at The Retreat while all about him the furniture was being packed up. They had decided to give up the place altogether. As usual in times of stress MacDonald fell ill, this time with pleurisy. In any case he had no money to pay his fare to Nervi. He had been relying on selling his latest book, *Paul Faber, Surgeon*, to Strahan, but Strahan, who was having financial difficulties, refused it as unsuitable for his *Day of Rest*. So MacDonald had to stay at The Retreat, where he had the consolation of a greater intimacy with Greville and Winifred, who were looking after him.

The Cowper-Temples came to his rescue. As soon as he was well enough to travel, they fetched him from the bare rooms and packing-cases to the comfort of their home in central London. Soon after, MacDonald was able to write to Louisa,

> William [Cowper-Temple] ... came in ... He said he wanted me to do him a favour: I was so pleased, thinking he really wanted me to do something for him. Then I cannot tell you how sweetly he begged me to take 'a few of his slates'—which were represented by a cheque for £200. I tried to refuse it—but it wouldn't do.[8]

Strahan offered to buy the copyright of *Paul Faber, Surgeon*, for £400—less than half what MacDonald had lately been getting for his novels. MacDonald accepted the offer. After paying all outstanding debts he had enough left over for the journey to Nervi and to keep the family that winter. Just before leaving England he had a letter from Lord Beaconsfield's secretary. It told him that he was to receive a Civil List pension of £100 a year. He had, the previous year, been presented to Princess Alice at Buckingham Palace; Mrs Cowper-Temple thought it was owing to her that he had been awarded the pension.

So they left The Retreat. William Morris took the place next, renaming it Kelmscott House. The neighbours, the two Misses Cobden, were sorry to see the change. 'With the Mac-Donalds' departure after eight years' residence there', Miss Anne was to write, 'the days of Christian Socialism came to an end at Hammersmith, to be succeeded for a time in the same house by the more strenuous days of Marxian Socialism.'[9]

The joyous reunion at the Palazzo Cattaneo was over-shadowed by the knowledge that Mary was dying. However, George and Louisa still did not neglect their friends. Octavia Hill was welcomed for a rest-cure in March 1878. She was worn out with her work among the poor, and smarting from the unjust criticism Ruskin had made of her in his periodical *Fors Clavigera*. MacDonald was naturally upset at this quarrel between two of his dearest friends. He had seen the article in *Fors Clavigera* and agreed that Octavia had been unfairly treated. News of Ruskin's nervous breakdown helped to explain his behaviour and to restore Octavia's confidence in his integrity; but it left her and MacDonald in some anxiety as to their friend's mental and spiritual health. As Mary Mac-Donald's health failed, Octavia left Nervi and went to Rome. Her sympathetic nature recoiled from intruding on the family's grief. Ted Hughes, Mary's fiancé, was sent for, and Mary died on 27 April 1878. Louisa in particular was grief-stricken. Her emotions had centred on the nursing of her child, and now that Mary was beyond her care, she could find no peace. The needs of her other offspring and of her husband, who fell ill once again, did not give her such a sense of purpose.

The Italian climate had done nothing for Mary, but it proved so beneficial to her father that the MacDonalds de-cided to have a permanent base there. They began to plan the building of a house to suit themselves, and in the meanwhile took the Villa Barratta (later the Hotel Splendide) at Porto-fino, near Rapallo. It was inaccessible by road, so that after getting off the train at Santa Margherita they had to complete the journey by rowing-boat.

In March 1879 young Maurice caught pneumonia. Mac-Donald wrote to Greville, then preparing for his final examination for the Royal College of Surgeons:

> Our Maurice is alive, but that is nearly all I can say... He has been sleeping a good deal today, and it seems as if he was gently gliding into the land where all is well. He is angelic—a poor word, but at least not too strong to express his patience and sweetness...
>
> I fear your mother will have a terrible illness when it is over; the fatigue is great, great... His brothers and sisters are just like strong angels tending a weak one...[10]

Maurice's condition was probably aggravated by tuberculosis; an abscess on the knee two years previously had been a warning of worse to come. He died after eighteen days' illness. 'He was just over fifteen', wrote his father to Carey Davies. 'It is a sore affliction, but though cast down we are not destroyed. Jesus rose again glorious, and to that I cleave fast.'[11]

Out of the sorrows of 1879 came *A Book of Strife, in the form of the Diary of an Old Soul*, which was published privately the following year. It is a long poem of 366 stanzas, one for each possible day of the year. In it MacDonald expressed his frustrations and anxieties, his constant feeling that his faith was too weak, and his longing for a vision of God to dispel his doubts:

> Have pity on us for the look of things
> When blank denial stares us in the face.
> Although the serpent-mask has lied before,
> It fascinates the bird that darkling sings,
> And numbs the little prayer-bird's beating wings.[12]

Above all else MacDonald was struggling to express his belief that Death was good. C. S. Lewis referred to 'a certain quality of death, *good* Death'[13] which he found in MacDonald's works. Over the years MacDonald had had to come to terms with the loss of his mother, brothers and father. Now that Death was taking his children too, his faith in the constancy of God's love and goodness received a challenge. Yet it was impossible to suppose that God loves and blesses at whim:

If to myself 'God sometimes interferes'
I said, my faith at once would be struck blind.[14]

His resolution of the dilemma was to see himself as a child who
does not know where to turn for the love which is always available:

I see a little child whose eager hands
Search the thick stream that drains the crowded street
For possible things hid in its current slow.
Near by, behind him, a great palace stands
Where kings might welcome nobles to their feet.
Soft sounds, sweet scents, fair sights there only go—
There the child's father lives, but the child does not know.

Oh, eager, hungry, busy-seeking child,
Rise up, turn round, run in, run up the stair:
Far in a chamber from the rude noise exiled,
Thy father sits, pondering how thou dost fare.
The mighty man will clasp thee to his breast;
Will kiss thee, stroke the tangles of thy hair,
And lap thee warm in fold on fold of lovely rest.[15]

Death was for him the last step towards home and Father, the
running up the stair, the prelude to a joyous meeting and a
glorious resurrection.

But he had to consider Death in this way for his children,
not just for himself. 'I want to be God's man, not the man of
my own idea', he wrote to Mrs Cowper-Temple shortly before
Mary died. 'I look forward—God grant I press forward too.
Parent could not have more comfort in his children than he
gives me in mine: shall I be oppressed because he may choose
to take one before the rest? Who knows how soon the turn of
her parents may come, and then they will be very glad she is
there and not here.'[16] His faith in the absolute sovereignty of
Divine Love led him to see that to grudge his children's deaths
would be to grudge them a taste of love, and to love them himself less than the best.

*

The family was cheered by the arrival of Richard Gilder, his wife and baby son. Gilder was making a tour of Europe as a convalescence after illness. He took his wife on to Pisa and Rome, leaving the little boy, Rodman (Rodboy, the MacDonalds called him), at Portofino for a short while.

The Italian air was good for MacDonald's mental powers as well as his physical condition. He was working on another novel, *Sir Gibbie*, the best of his Scottish stories, though almost impenetrable in places with its Scottish dialect. In the well-remembered setting of Aberdeen's slums MacDonald places Sir Gibbie, the pure child, who grows from innocence to righteousness in spite of his environment, his dumbness and his drunken father. In case readers should find Gibbie too good to be true MacDonald wrote

> the loudest demand of the present day is for the representation of that grade of humanity of which men see the most.... But whatever the demand of the age, I insist that that which *ought* to be presented to its beholding, is the common good uncommonly developed, and that not because of its rarity, but because it is truer to humanity.[17]

Sir Gibbie was published simultaneously in England and America in 1879, and was serialised in *The Glasgow Weekly Mail*. Among enthusiastic readers was the future Bishop of Adelaide, George Kennion. Greville MacDonald met him several years later on a voyage to the Far East. He wrote to his mother:

> I have just had *such* a talk with the Bishop. I found him on deck after dinner working the punkah to relieve the little nigger who had been at it all dinner time. So I began to talk to him. Soon he asked me if I were related to George MacDonald. I said he was my father ... He told me that it was reading *Sir Gibbie* that made him refuse a very rich London living that was offered him, although he was poor—a very different thing, he said, from a Colonial Bishopric.[18]

Where *Sir Gibbie* is especially Scottish, *Paul Faber, Surgeon* is particularly English. It too was published in 1879; it seems that Strahan could not afford the publishing costs and sold the copyright to Hurst & Blackett. MacDonald recalled his Arundel days in this novel, not only in his description of the town 'Glaston', but also in his treatment of Mr Drake, the Congregational minister who is shabbily pensioned off by his deacons. The book's main theme, however, is self-honesty, the need to face up to and understand one's lower nature. The two main characters, Paul Faber and his wife Juliet, both need to learn to face themselves. They each have had a love-affair before their marriage, which both are trying to bury in oblivion. Juliet breaks down first, and confesses to Paul. In his self-righteous indignation he rejects her.

To emphasise the concept of the lower nature MacDonald uses animals as symbols. At the centre of the book he has Thomas Wingfold, his most authoritative character, say

> Let us each remember that we carry in us the characteristics of each and every animal. . . . Except the living Father have brought order, harmony, a world, out of his chaos, a man is but a cage of unclean beasts, with no-one to rule them.[19]

This is clear when we see Juliet fleeing from Paul in much the same way as a dog, experimented on by Faber's assistant, rushes in pain and terror from Faber's door. And Paul in his injured pride is represented by his red horse Ruber, which he rides desperately and wildly the morning after Juliet's confession. He has a bad fall, the horse is killed and Paul injured. Then he is humiliated by the discovery that his illegitimate daughter is being cared for locally, and he has to admit to himself that he is worse than Juliet. His own affair and his insensitivity of conscience were bad enough; worse than that, he had the presumption to condemn Juliet for a similar lapse!

Once they have faced the bitter truth about themselves the way is clear for a reconciliation. A new and surer relationship is possible, based on honesty and self-knowledge. MacDonald gives an example of such a marriage in this novel, in the relationship between Thomas and Helen Wingfold. In contrast with the Fabers, they are honest in every way, and their marriage is one of love, trust and joy. MacDonald shows Helen's control over her lower nature symbolically, with the two tiny ponies Zephyr and Zoe ('wind or spirit' and 'life'), which draw

137

her carriage. She has a perfect intuitive control over them, and, moreover, uses them to bring joy to others: she gives all the village children rides in the carriage, 'to the glory of God'.

*

The MacDonalds still thought of England as their home. They intended to return in the summer, to see friends, for George to give lectures, and for *The Pilgrim's Progress* to be performed. Louisa wrote to Carey Davies in April 1879:

> I wonder whether you will be surprised to hear that we are intend-ing to act our Bunyan's *Pilgrim's Progress* wherever we can. We have already made four engagements, the results of which will pay—and more—our journey home. But then we must have some more in order to pay our journey back... *The Pilgrims* has [become] such a reality to us that it seems a *duty* to do it—from the multitude of *testimonies* we have had to the moral and good of the play.[20]

It seems that *The Pilgrim's Progress*, once begun, could not be stopped. Even MacDonald himself was coming to be respected by his friends as much for his part as Mr Greatheart as for his writing; yet he did not cease writing. He was often correcting proofs as he sat in the wings awaiting his cue. Greville had nothing to do with the acting now that he had started his own medical practice. Robert was studying as an architect and could help in the summer holidays, as could Ronald after he had started at Oxford University in 1882. They took on the publicity and management side of the productions.

The Lord Chancellor refused to licence a religious play. Some of the MacDonalds' friends and relations agreed that to use the stage for a religious presentation was sacrilegious. MacDonald took the opposite view; he considered the objec-tion superstitious and therefore heathenish. Louisa always found means to circumvent the law, by arranging for perform-ances to be given in private houses. She used curtains (some still in existence, with appliqué designs of birds and flowers) in place of scenery. Not only *The Pilgrim's Progress* but also *Mac-beth* and Corneille's *Polyeucte* were performed. Until 1887 every summer was spent in this way.

Lilia had many admirers of her acting, but one old lady disapproved. Lilia was in love with this lady's nephew and he with her; but the old lady, whose heir he was, refused to sanction the marriage unless Lilia promised never to act in public. For Lilia, to repudiate her art would have been a denial of her faith. She had learned from her father to see art as a means of elevating and educating people:

> the pictures and objects of art of all kinds [MacDonald had written] with which a man adorns the house he has chosen or built to live in, have thenceforward not a little to do with the education of his tastes and feelings. Even when he is not aware of it, they are working upon him for good, if he has chosen what is good.[21]

What her father felt about the visual arts, Lilia applied to drama, and as a result she refused to stop acting. Her suitor, unwilling to lose his aunt's estate, persisted in his attempts to persuade Lilia to give up her vocation. In the end she had to sever the relationship. She devoted herself more than ever to the service of friends and family—a devotion that was eleven years later to cost her her life.

The summers' hard work, for which, according to Greville MacDonald, 'not one of the company was physically fit',[22] had its reward in the Italian winters. The plan for the MacDonalds' own house came to fruition, largely owing to the generosity of Princess Alice, the Mount-Temples, the Mathesons, Octavia Hill and her sisters, and many others. A site was bought at Bordighera (they were returning to the Riviera) and a house was built to MacDonald's design. It was named Casa Coraggio—'Corage' again! It had an enormous living room, 52 feet by 26 feet by 13 feet high. A third of it was curtained off as a dining room. In 1891 a two-manual pipe organ was installed in the dining room. It was the bequest of Louisa's brother George, who died the previous year. The house was the realisation of a dream for MacDonald, and, naturally, it stimulated him to fresh flights of fancy.

> My father [writes Greville] ... was an unflinching idealist. With his new home at Bordighera at last built and furnished, his hope was that like some chief of a clan, he might keep his children near

him, whatever their work. One son was to be a doctor, the second a schoolmaster, the third an architect. The fourth son Maurice, who had died at Porto Fino in 1879, would it had been hoped, do great things for the Church, even though bishoprics were none too plentiful on the Riviera. If I write jestingly, it is in all reverence, knowing it was only the paternal love for us that, now and again, conceived such happy impossibilities.[23]

In the new house the MacDonalds held 'At Homes' on Wednesday afternoons, at which George would read and expound his favourite literature. On Sunday evenings they held informal services, with the big room holding about a hundred worshippers. Louisa played the organ and had some members of the local English church choir, which she had trained and built up, to sing anthems and hymns. Greville describes the scene when, at eight o'clock, his father 'with his white head and beard, his searching blue eyes, his crimson velvet cap' would enter the room and take his seat by the open fire. There were

> two candles on a little gate-legged table before him, the red glow of the olive logs occasionally breaking into flame and lighting up the green and red tiles, just as his words of fire leapt into flaming life an drove out the dark shadows from our souls... At last my father would, perhaps quite unexpectedly, rise and kneel, so that all ... must feel their hearts opening out to God... And then came a blessing, wonderful in its quiet, deeply penetrating, almost tremulous words ... then a deep silence, and perhaps the great organ softly rolling forth Handel's Largo... Still and quiet even now, the guests would at last rise and go down the wide stone stair and out beneath the flashing stars of the huge Italian sky.[24]

Despite all his lecturing, preaching, acting and entertaining, MacDonald somehow found time to continue writing. *Mary Marston* was published in 1881, a novel dealing with class-consciousness. Once again MacDonald claims that true greatness is measured in terms of love and service, not by wealth or rank. Along with this 'society' novel he was working on a Scottish story with a strong 'Gothic' feel, *Castle Warlock*. *Weighed and Wanting*, published in 1882, pursued the 'society' theme. Scenes from middle-class London life are also included in *The*

Gifts of the Christ Child, a collection of short stories. 'The But-cher's Bills' is perhaps the first story ever to deal with post-natal depression. Typically, MacDonald sees it as having spiritual as well as physical causes.

MacDonald now had various pieces of writing which had accumulated over the years, and in 1882 he collected them all together in two volumes. He selected new stories and descrip-tive pieces and included them in a new edition of *Adela Cath-cart*, in place of the stories which had become so well known. He published thirteen essays and sermons in the collection en-titled *Orts* (an old word meaning 'scraps'). Perhaps at this period he was busy tidying up and fastening off loose ends. At any rate, he arranged for the publication in book form of *The Princess and Curdie*, which had so far only appeared as a serial, and wrote a sequel to *Sir Gibbie, Donal Grant*. This is delight-fully melodramatic, with a wicked earl, a bricked-up chapel with a skeleton, and ghostly moanings at night. MacDonald believed in ghosts, but he was careful to give most of his ghost-ly manifestations a rational explanation. He based his 'Morven Castle' on Fyvie Castle, about which Carey Davies sent him a newscutting. MacDonald replied,

> Thank you for the newspaper cutting. I wish I had read it before *Donal Grant* . . .
> I knew it was a grand stair; I have a passion for stairs; for I have a photograph of an engraving of it given me by the widow of the last owner but one . . .
> I am told there is a disused avenue at Glamis like the one I have in the book. Of that I had not the glimmer of an idea. All I knew of it was the story of the devil and the card-players which I had heard as a child . . .[25]

In sorting out his papers MacDonald may have rediscovered the poems of Greville Matheson and of John MacDonald. He put them together with some of his own and published the col-lection as *A Threefold Cord* in 1883. It was dedicated to Greville MacDonald, to his great delight.

To a modern ear MacDonald's poetry is not quite success-ful. It lacks the density and conciseness we associate with the best poetry. This may be because he was heavily influenced by the ballad, a form he had known from early childhood. In the ballad, rhyme and rhythm dominate over the telling line, the significant phrase. So in MacDonald's poetry lines that in themselves say very little are slipped in for the sake of the metre. The third line in the following stanza, for example, is nothing but padding:

> Babe Jesus lay in Mary's lap,
> The sun shone in his hair;
> And this was how she saw, mayhap,
> The crown already there.[26]

And sometimes even his rhythms sound uncomfortably uneven, as in the first two stanzas of 'A Song in the Night':

> I would I were an angel strong,
> An angel of the sun, hasting along!
>
> I would I were just come awake,
> A child outbursting from night's dusty brake![27]

The demands of the sonnet form, however, helped to amend MacDonald's tendency to looseness of diction, and some of his best poems are sonnets. 'The Unseen Face', which is about Moses' vision of God, suggests in terse and powerful language that the God of Sinai is also the suffering Christ of Calvary:

> From Sinai's top, the vaporous, thunderous place,
> God passed in cloud, an earthy garment worn
> To hide, and thus reveal. In love, not scorn,
> He put him in a clift of the rock's base,
> Covered him with his hand, his eyes to screen—
> Passed—lifted it: his back alone appears!
> Ah, Moses, had he turned, and hadst thou seen
> The pale face crowned with thorns, baptized with tears,
> The eyes of the true man, by men belied,
> Thou hadst beheld God's face, and straightway died![28]

As is to be expected of MacDonald, where he succeeds best as a poet is in the elucidation of images. He takes an idea, a symbol, and works it out in verse so that, regardless of his diction, it is the picture, not the poem, that stays with the reader. In 'Lycabas', for example,[29] he begins with the notion that the

142

months of the year are twelve wolves. They pursue him and harry him and take his dearest lambs. But when they have chased him right to the shepherd's feet he recognises them for sheep-dogs, sent to bring him home. Thus in vivid symbols MacDonald shows how the passing of time can be seen as a blessing, not a curse.

*

In the autumn of 1883 Greville accompanied his parents to Casa Coraggio. He was seeking to establish a general practice, and decided to serve the community at Bordighera, using a room on the ground floor of his father's house as a surgery. The enterprise failed, however, for not enough people would pay him for his services. He had his compensations, nevertheless:

> those few months had their pleasures, though the most memorable are the hours with my father in his study. I began once more to read the Greek Testament with him. We talked much—so fine a listener was he!—and I realised how and why the Gospel's message was to him, and must become to all men, Life and the only secret of more life.
>   . . . in spite of having the run of his large, richly various library, I learned more from contact with my father than from all his books. Nor were we by any means always and entirely in agreement, even if in perfect understanding.[30]

Greville moved to Florence with Lilia to assist and keep house, but failed yet again to establish himself. He was becoming depressed, and his parents anxious on his behalf. Greville believed that his deafness was at the root of both failures, for it made a good bedside manner extremely difficult to achieve. He thought, too, that his parents 'never quite realised how much I was physically handicapped, and were troubled at my apparent vacillation'.[31]

1884 was turning out to be a difficult year for MacDonald, for on top of his anxiety over his son was the greater grief caused by the death of his third daughter Grace. She died of tuberculosis, leaving a two-year-old daughter, Octavia, to console her grandparents. Then there was the continually

143

renewed strain of the summer's acting and lecturing tour. The toll was always heaviest in September, when MacDonald would cram in as many lectures as possible before his return to Italy. It is not altogether surprising that no new books were published in this year.

10

Last words: 1884–1905

In 1885 MacDonald published *The Tragedie of Hamlet*, a scholarly edition of the First Folio, with Second Quarto variant readings, together with his own notes. MacDonald's understanding of Shakespeare was ethical rather than dramatic, and he interpreted the characters in moral terms. As *Macbeth* was a study in cowardice, so *Hamlet* is a picture of moral courage. MacDonald wrote of Hamlet,

> They call it weakness that he would not, foolishly and selfishly, make good his succession against the king, regardless of the law of election, and careless of the weal of the kingdom for which he shows himself so anxious even in the throes of death! To my mind he is the grandest hero in fiction—absolutely human—so troubled, yet so true![1]

The preparation of this edition may have coincided with a series of lectures on Shakespeare at Casa Coraggio. Edmund Maurice attended one on the Sonnets and another on *Julius Caesar*,

> in which he compared Caesar to the more bragging kind of Irishman. Unfortunately there was an Irishman present; but he was quite pacified at the end by the lecturer saying he himself was a Highlander and therefore liable to the same Celtic temptation.[2]

(MacDonald often used to say, 'If anyone tells me it is an easy thing to speak the truth, I should tell him that he had never tried it'.)[3]

The big room at Casa Coraggio was also used for special Christmas displays. Louisa had the idea of dressing up members of the family to represent medieval pictures of the Nativity in *tableaux vivants*. They were done using the simplest of

145

materials and lighting, with the most beautiful effects. Lord Mount-Temple wrote about his visit to Bordighera one Christmas:

> On Christmas eve ... we heard the sound of many voices, and looking out, lamps glimmered among the trees, and [we saw] figures carrying lanterns and sheets of music. Who should they be but the dear MacDonald family visiting the houses of all the invalids in the place, to sing them carols...
>
> Sometimes there were concerts and theatricals for our amusement or for charity, and this winter there was a concert for the completion of the church for the poor of the Marina. This delighted the good Father Giacomo, the village priest, as a mark of true Christian feeling and catholicity.[4]

MacDonald had an excellent relationship with Padre Giacomo, who would embrace him if he met him walking along the road. There were a few in the English community at Bordighera who frowned on MacDonald's sympathy with the Roman Catholics. He was only doing as he had always done, loving those who loved his Lord, in a truly ecumenical spirit.

At Christmas times Casa Coraggio was always full of guests. As at The Retreat George and Louisa 'adopted' people in particular need. In 1881 Louisa had taken in two little girls and then their mother, who was dying of tuberculosis but rallied and spent seven years as one of the family at Bordighera. A friend of Lilia's came to stay, also suffering from tuberculosis. Household expenses were heavy; some guests would contribute to the MacDonald funds, but only the most intimate friends were allowed to do so. As MacDonald wrote to an admirer, returning her cheque,

> an obligation ought to be a sweet thing, like a scent of old rose-leaves, to be carried in one's soul to all eternity— a bond of ever-growing union—not a burden which one keeps ever hitching on the other shoulder because he cannot to all Eternity get rid of it.[5]

Guests were amazed at the splendid hospitality the MacDonalds offered them with so little money. The secret was that the girls had inherited their mother's ability to make wonderful things out of next to nothing. Similarly with entertainment; Louisa had a genius for parties. On one occasion she and

George sent invitations in doggerel verse: they and their guests would celebrate New Year's Eve with dancing; if everyone brought a combustible item they could start with a bonfire!

The MacDonald hospitality was tried to the limit in February 1887, when Northern Italy was struck by a severe earthquake. Louisa described it to Anna Leigh-Smith:

> An earthquake yesterday morning, about six o'clock, surprised us out of our beds ... The poor people have suffered the most—their houses came tumbling about their ears, some buried in the ruins. Our plaster cracked and ceilings and vases and jugs broken—but our walls, so well built, stood firm—the only danger to us is from the stupid stucco tower that I daresay you remember vexed us so—George having ordered the tower to be of the same stone as the rest of the house. However, it received such a shock yesterday that it will have to be taken down.[6]

The houses of the English suffered less than those of the Italians, as they were on the whole more strongly built. 'The English about us have suffered not at all', wrote Lilia to a friend, 'and in some cases have behaved disgracefully'—unlike the MacDonalds, who housed as many of the homeless as they could in the circumstances, and held sewing parties to make clothes 'for people whose every rag is buried'.[7] The day after the first shock, Louisa was sitting at the organ in the church, escaping for a few moments from the chaos at Casa Coraggio, when there was another fierce shock. The whole building swayed and shook, and seemed likely to collapse. Louisa was equal to the occasion; she recklessly pulled out all the stops and played the Hallelujah Chorus! The shocks continued for about two weeks. The inmates of Casa Coraggio spent the worst days out of doors, all except George. He stayed in his study, writing. His books were flung all over the floor, although, amazingly, a little figure of Christ remained in its place on the top of a bookcase.

MacDonald was to include a powerful description of the earthquake in his next book for children, *A Rough Shaking*. Meanwhile he was using a Scottish background for the settings of his novels *What's Mine's Mine* and *The Elect Lady*. It was a mark of the respect in which he was widely held that he was asked to write prefaces for the books of others. He wrote two: one to *For the Right* by Karl Emil Franzos, in which he discussed his concept of art. He reiterated what he had written in *Sir Gibbie*, at the same time taking note of contemporary views of art:

> The cry of 'Art for art's sake', as a protest against the pursuit of art for the sake of money or fame, one can recognise in its half wisdom, knowing the right cry to be 'Art for truth's sake!' But when certain writers tell us that the true aim of the author of fiction is to give people what they want, namely, a reflection, as in a mirror, of themselves—a mirror not such as will show them to themselves as they are, but as they seem to each other, some of us feel that we stand on the verge of an abyss of falsehood.[8]

He also wrote the preface to *Letters from Hell* by V. A. Thisted. Many people thought that MacDonald himself was the author of this work, although its pictures of hell are too concrete, not symbolic enough to be from MacDonald's pen. In the preface he addressed himself to those who had misunderstood his own teaching:

> Thousands of half-thinkers imagine that, since it is declared with such authority that hell is not everlasting, there is then no hell at all. To such folly I for one have never given enticement or shelter. I see no hope for many, no way for the divine love to reach them, save through a very ghastly hell. Men have got to repent; there is no other escape for them, and no escape from that.[9]

Besides the gatherings of many friends about George and Louisa, there were also sad partings. Lord Mount-Temple died in England in 1888. During his last illness he would complain half-seriously that his wife's prayers for his recovery were delaying his deliverance from this world and his entry into the next. Ronald was married that summer, and travelled with his wife to the United States, where he took a post as headmaster of an Episcopalian boys' school in Asheville, North Carolina. His wife died two years later. Lilia went out to keep house for him and to cheer him up as much as she could. In a letter to her, MacDonald spoke of his work:

> the attempt to speak what I mean is the same kind of failure that

walking is—a mere, constantly recurring recovery from falling . . .
I have still one *great* poem in my mind, but it will never be written, I think, except we have a fortune left us, so that I need not
write any more stories—of which I am beginning to be tired . . .[10]

If MacDonald was getting tired of fiction, it did not show in his
work. He was to write half a dozen more stories before finally
laying down his pen. He had published a second volume of *Unspoken Sermons* in 1885, and in 1889 he produced the third and
final series. It dealt in a mature and profound manner with
basic concepts of the Kingdom such as Freedom, Justice,
Light and Righteousness. In 1892 he published *The Hope of the
Gospel*, a return to his best love, the work and words of Jesus.
The final sermon of this volume, 'The Hope of the Universe',
was published in an expanded form in *Sunday Magazine*, and in
1896 an abridged version of this was published for the benefit
of the Victoria Street Society for the Protection of Animals
from Vivisection. MacDonald was strongly opposed to any
form of cruelty to animals. He supported Ruskin in his opposition to vivisection (in March 1885 Ruskin had resigned his
Slade Professorship in protest at the Oxford University authorities building a new physiology laboratory in which experi-
ments on animals would take place), and in *Paul Faber, Surgeon*,
had included a sermon against such practices. He wrote about
animals, too, in *A Rough Shaking*, which came out in 1890.
Clare Skymer, who has lost his parents in an earthquake, has a
rare ability to make friends with the beasts. Like Gibbie, Clare
is an innocent. He is considered by many to be mentally
deranged because of his moral rectitude. MacDonald shows
in the story that worldly normality is in fact 'deranged' and
that Clare's values are those of the only true man, Jesus
Christ.

In *There and Back*, published in 1891, MacDonald took up
once again a 'society' theme and explored the effects of environment and education on the individual. *The Flight of the
Shadow* was a return to the simple narrative style of *The Portent*,
and included some powerful images, with a startling dénouement in Versailles' Hall of Mirrors. The mirror was an important symbol for MacDonald of man's discovery of himself. He

was familiar with many references in literature, from the clouded mirror of St Paul's 'now we see in a glass darkly' to the mirror of the Lady of Shalott, in Tennyson's poem, in which she sees her ideal. MacDonald had included, in the middle of *Phantastes*, a story about a young man who sees and falls in love with the lady in a magic mirror, a story which parallels the tale of Anodos and his search for his Ideal.

Social and family life, always so important to George and Louisa, continued to occupy and stimulate them. George's cousin Margaret Troup had three sons, Charles, Francis and James. Charles and Francis often visited Bordighera, and Charles had spent some vacations as tutor to the younger Mac-Donald boys, Bernard and MacKay. The two young men were present at the Christmas festivities of 1890. To judge by this letter from Francis to James, they had a splendid time:

> There is a party of 20 of us in the house—so you may guess there's some fun and lots of nonsense. There's one jolly little girl with the reddest hair I ever saw. MacKay and I are both gone on her and I have had some narrow escapes with my life through my successful efforts to excite his jealousy...
>
> You see we have been at lots of picnics and drives and when not at that at long tramps in the hills. Saw last Sunday a little town perched on top of a hill near 3000 ft high—church on the apex all in ruins lying just as it fell in the earthquake when 200 people were killed in it [this was destroyed in the earthquake of 1887 which damaged Casa Coraggio]. They have just built another new place lower down the hill...
>
> We dress for dinner every night which is nice when you are used to it. Play cards mostly after dinner. You have heard me 'do the hen' I suppose. Cousin George is immensely fond of it and made me perform to a great company—in fact we had a regular farm-yard. I was regarded as a grand success and something like a party was invited one evening to have a repetition of it. A brilliant idea occurred to me in the interval, which MacKay and I carried out successfully and with enormous éclat. I sung (sung—by george—what d'ye think of that?) sung 'Ye banks and braes' but as if done by a *hen*. Cousin George nearly split himself laughing. I stuck about the last line and to finish ran in to 'The keel row' à la chickie, which was if anything an improvement. I was encored and instead of trying another I apologised in Hen language—you never heard

such a farce in all your born days—and there I was going about Bordighera meeting people at every turn who saw me making a perfect idiot of myself.[11]

After the break up of the Christmas party Lilia returned from America. Ronald was in much better spirits, and had found a cousin to do his housekeeping. Lilia's friend—the one who had joined the Bordighera household on account of tuberculosis—was much worse and needed her. By this time the infectiousness of the disease was fully realised by medical science. With Greville a doctor and MacKay a medical student, Lilia could not be unaware of the danger she ran; nevertheless she gave herself unreservedly to the care of her friend in her last days. After the friend's death, early in 1891, Lilia showed signs of having contracted the disease. The family came to England and rented Stock Rectory, Billericay, for the summer, while George made his last lecture tour. Surprisingly, considering his age (67) and his medical history, he was in good health and able to enjoy his work. He took the opportunity to visit Huntly, and stayed with his cousin James at The Farm. James took him to Ruthven, the setting for *The Wow o' Rivven*. He described the outing in a letter to Louisa:

> I have been out for a few miles' drive—to the old church of Ruthven, of which only the gable and belfry remain, with a beautiful old bell... Right at the foot of the belfry the fool of my story lies buried, with a gravestone set up by the people of Huntly telling about him, and how he thought that bell, now above his body, always said, 'Come hame, come hame.'[12]

Louisa took Lilia back to Bordighera before MacDonald had finished his tour. They were afraid she would be too ill to travel if they waited, and they could not stay in Billericay indefinitely. George wrote to Louisa from North Wales,

> She has never taken care of herself, and now we must take care of her. If it should please God to leave her, we shall all take care of her; if not, we shall find her soon at the farthest.... A great good is coming to us all—too big for this world to hold.[13]

In her reply from Casa Coraggio Louisa wrote,

Knowing all I do now of what unintentional agonies we have made
our children suffer, all the while having a heart full of love and intended good-will to them, I could not *dare*, of my choice, have over
again such a lovely family as was given to us to rear and teach and
guide.[14]

MacDonald left England in the first week of November. He
had given forty-eight lectures in fifty-eight days. 'My work is
done', he said, and never again spoke in public for a fee. Before
he left London he paid a last visit to William Matheson, who
died on 21 November. Lilia died on the 22nd, in her father's
arms. She was 39 years old. Greville described her funeral:

When the coffin was carried into the church the congregation
joined in the singing... The tremulous, subdued voices showed
how deeply everyone was mourning the loss of a cherished friend,
that woman who, from her very childhood, had been a mother to
old and young. Her father could hardly leave the grave: he came
back twice after all others had left, and it was with difficulty he was
at last led away.[15]

Nothing could be the same after Lilia's death. 1891 marked,
as it were, the beginning of the end. Louisa in particular began
to show a marked deterioration in health. She had for a long
time had an enlarged thyroid gland, which the climate of the
Riviera had not helped. She became increasingly nervous and
moody. Her condition affected her vocal cords, reducing her
breathing. She consulted her son, now a successful nose and
throat specialist (he found his deafness much less of a drawback in this field), who assured his mother and father that
everything was all right. Greville knew her condition was inop-
erable but felt it right to deceive his parents. He later wrote,

My father, I well knew, would never sanction such deception,
especially if a *yea* or *nay* had been required. Once I put it to him
that sometimes one had to choose between a calamitous shock
from the literal truth and a merciful falsehood. He argued that a
permissible equivocation would meet any case. Nevertheless, such
a loophole would be hardly more honest and might be even more
harmful than the truth. In the case of my mother, my fearless
untruth did wonders for her.[16]

It probably saved his father a lot of heartache too.

With no need to return to England now the lectures were finished, George and Louisa could spend the summer of 1892 at Arth in Switzerland. It was a quiet holiday, for Louisa in particular could not get about very much without the help of a bath-chair. Around midsummer George finished another novel, *Heather and Snow*, but by that time he was feeling his age. He wrote to Carey Davies,

> I have no impulse toward public work this year. I do not think I should feel at all sorry if I were told I should never preach or lecture again. Somehow I have very little feeling of doing good that way. But let everything always be as our Father wills.[17]

By the New Year MacDonald was finding life burdensome. Every week he gave his literary readings, with commentary, but it was becoming more and more of an effort. 'Bordighera keeps advancing in the loss of its virtues and repose', he wrote to Greville. 'We shall be compelled, I fear, to open our doors only half-way before long.'[18] It seems the place was becoming more of a commercialised resort and less of a haven for the MacDonalds.

Heather and Snow was published in 1893. In it MacDonald explored the idea of insanity which he had touched on in *A Rough Shaking*. Steenie Barclay is a congenital idiot; MacDonald gives a striking picture of his condition, together with his sister Kirstie's loving care of him. As in the earlier work *The Wow o' Rivven* he suggests that the commonplace, unspiritual man is really the 'idiot'. Steenie sees angels walking over the Scottish moors, together with Jesus Christ, 'the bonny man' as Steenie calls him: 'Doubtless, what kept him lord of himself through all the truth-aping delusions that usurped his consciousness, was his unyielding faith in the bonny man.'[19] MacDonald had long been interested in the workings of the unconscious mind. His son Greville had spent a period of his medical training as an assistant in a mental hospital, and had no doubt shared his experiences with his father. The insane person's idiosyncratic view of the seen and the unseen worlds fascinated MacDonald. He believed that a true vision of the

Son of God could do wonders in achieving cures; Steenie in the novel not only keeps himself 'lord of himself' but actually improves in his mental condition.

It is possible that in *Heather and Snow* MacDonald was attempting to exorcise a fear that was to grow on him as the months passed. Five years later he would be asking Louisa for reassurance that his own wits had not all gone. In 1893, however, he had not lost his powers. He was still greatly sought-after, and had to write to his literary agent,

> Dear Watt,
>   I can't do it, even to oblige you. . . . I never have and never will consent to be interviewed. I will do *nothing* to bring my personality before the public in any way farther than my work in itself necessitates.[20]

MacDonald fought shy of admirers. To an autograph-hunter he had written this:

> Seek not my name—it doth no virtue bear;
>   Seek, seek thine own primeval name to find—
> The name God called when thy ideal fair
>   Arose in deeps of the eternal mind.
>
> When that thou findest, thou art straight a lord
>   Of time and space—art heir of all things grown;
> And not my name, poor, earthly label-word,
>   But I myself thenceforward am thine own.[21]

There are not many people who can reject public acclaim and the cult of personality. MacDonald did not avoid public interest altogether—his career as a lecturer demonstrates how well he related to people *en masse*—but he hated the superficiality of hero-worship. His relationships with people had to be real and deep. He wanted friends, not admirers.

*

Back in 1890 MacDonald had begun a story—a fantasy—which he felt was inspired directly by God. The first draft was, unusually for him, largely free from alterations, and showed every sign of inspirational pressure, flowing from page to page with few breaks for paragraphs, and little punctuation. This was the first version of *Lilith*. In 1893 and '94 he typed out the story and at this stage made substantial revisions, though without altering the symbols in it.

Despite the fluency with which it came to him, MacDonald was working under severe emotional stress. He was deeply anxious about Greville, who was going through a period of spiritual trial. Unfortunately Greville himself gives only the vaguest hints as to the nature of this trial, and adds that his father misunderstood the situation. What is clear, however, is that MacDonald supposed his eldest son was giving way to some sort of temptation. It was agony for him to think that he would be estranged from his son and no longer able to trust him—for this is what was at stake. He wrote *Lilith* partly as a warning to Greville never to compromise with evil.

Vane, the hero of *Lilith*, wants to help the people of the world in which he finds himself, but does not know that the best way to do good lies in obedience. He is told that he must enter the House of Death, to sleep there; but he is reluctant and insists on doing 'good', and on doing it in his own way. All his well-meaning efforts end in disaster for those he is trying to help, until at last he consents to lie down and sleep. It is too easy, says MacDonald to his son, to deceive yourself into following the appearance of good, to do wrong believing that the outcome will justify the act. The real good is harder to accomplish, for it involves inner self-denial, not outward acts of heroism.

In *Lilith* MacDonald shows many different aspects of evil, from the naked horror of the monstrous phantasms that assail Vane in the Bad Burrow, through the terrifying aggression of the combatants in the Evil Wood, to the seductive beauty of Lilith, the spotted princess who preys on her people and on Vane. Vane also encounters goodness in strange and unlikely characters. Lona, Lilith's daughter, with her people the Lovers, helps and befriends him. Mara, the Lady of Bitterness with her white leopardess, seems evil at first, but as Vane discovers is a true friend to him and to Lilith. Hardest of all for Vane to realise is that the House of Death which is kept and warded by Adam and Eve is not a cold charnel house but a place of sweet sleep and beautiful dreams. He has to learn by painful experience to distinguish between true good and evil.

When Vane has at last discovered his rightful place in Adam's house, he has a fresh problem. He dreams that he is awake and active, sometimes in the strange world of Lilith and Mara, sometimes in the real world. How is he to tell when he is really awake and when he is asleep? He puts the problem to Adam, who explains that until he has slept the sleep of Death and woken up fully Dead—and then most truly Alive—, until then everything will be more or less a dream: 'When you are quite dead, you will dream no false dream. The soul that is true can generate nothing that is not true, neither can the false enter it.'[22] The true and full awakening, then, comes after death, in the world of eternity. Meanwhile MacDonald, through Vane, grapples with the question of the quality of life here and now. If life is a dream, of what value is it? Can dreams and aspirations have any purpose? Can a lovely dream be better than a dreary reality? MacDonald's answer is that loveliness is not necessarily an indication of falsehood. Dreams and ideals should not be rejected as too good to be true, but recognised as gifts from God and therefore of immense value: 'When a man dreams his own dream, he is the sport of his dream; when Another gives it him, that Other is able to fulfil it.'[23] MacDonald closes the book with his favourite quotation from Novalis: 'Our life is no dream, but it should and will perhaps become one.'[24]

When the book was completed and Louisa read the manuscript, she was bothered by its strangeness, and did not want it published. Greville, by this time restored to his parents' confidence, was asked to help:

> For the first time in their life [wrote Greville] they were at variance. Then they determined that I should adjudicate. To me, my father wrote, apropos of its difficulties, 'I am so tired of everything; yet with oh! so much to learn; and trouble the only way.'[25]

Greville found *Lilith* enthralling, called it 'The Revelation of St. George', and recommended publication. Chatto & Windus did not feel they could offer for this fantasy the usual high remuneration MacDonald's books could command; not that this in itself troubled him. His financial situation was assured since 1893, when Greville made arrangements to give him a regular pension, but it added to his general feeling of depression and failure. It seems as if the writing of *Lilith* had exhausted him in a way no other book had done. He wrote to Greville,

> I have been and still am going through a time of trial. That my book is not to be a success in the money way is not much of a trial, thanks to you; but the conscious failing—the doubt if I shall ever write another book—is a trial that stirs up other mental and spiritual trials, one being the great dread of becoming a burden.
>
> But God may have some relief in store for me, and work seems a little more probable to me, and I have got some good in having my pride brought down a little... But an eternal ripeness may well take many suns and frosts... Next Dec. I shall be 70... I am glad at the thought of being so near Home now.[26]

Lilith came out in 1895 and attracted little notice. The public had become used to MacDonald's novels and disliked *Lilith*'s return to the symbolic style of *Phantastes*, though it had greater depth and maturity. Ironically, *Phantastes* and *Lilith* have survived, though the novels have gone out of print.

Lilith was to be MacDonald's last great work. The heat of composition, coupled with his anxiety about Greville, caused insomnia and an increase in his eczema. Greville was later able to establish conclusively that the eczema varied with his father's emotional state, and that 'certain letters of mine were all unwittingly yet definitely responsible for now increase, now mitigation of the misery.'[27] In his early seventies MacDonald was able to cope with the pain and tiredness he was suffering; in fact, he deliberately set himself a course of reading and study in the hope of distracting his mind from the constant discomfort, and of stimulating it to rise above the tiredness. He read Spanish, Italian, Dutch and German as well as English, and preferred books that taxed his mind. He was determined to keep his brain active, to withstand the senility of which he had a lurking fear.

The English community at Bordighera was, as we have seen, becoming less and less congenial to him, and he had withdrawn from many of its activities. Nevertheless, in the winter of 1896–7, he was roused to speak out with his old fire and vigour in a way which endeared him to his fellow country-men. Dr Goodchild, doctor to the community and a close friend of MacDonald's, was accused of libelling an Italian doctor, and members of the MacDonald family were required to give evidence. MacDonald himself, furious at the absurdity of the accusation, defended his friend with hot indignation, and the charge was dropped. The Bordighera community was loud in MacDonald's praises. But once the moment of anger was over that had so stimulated him, MacDonald was deeply unhappy. He felt that such 'fulgurous wrath' (as Ronald Mac-Donald would have called it) was very wrong and merited only self-reproach.

Thus, the late 1890s were characterised by a slow-growing depression exacerbated by insomnia and eczema. It was held at bay by periods of hard academic and creative work, and by the stimulation afforded through human relationships. Mac-Donald did manage two last works: his last full-length novel, *Salted with Fire*, was published in 1897. Remembering his Scot-tish origins MacDonald wrote of the hypocrisy and repentance of a young minister in a Scottish town. His very last story, 'Far Above Rubies', which was published in the Christmas number of *The Sketch* 1898, was also a memory of early days, as well as being a tribute to Louisa. It is a tale about a young writer struggling to establish himself; his morale is boosted by his wife's love and courage.

If this work was actually penned early in 1898 it probably coincided with a last resurgence of the old life and gaiety at Casa Coraggio. In the spring a friend of Greville's stayed at Bordighera with the MacDonalds. William Nicoll, Professor of Singing at the Royal Academy of Music, sent the following account to the Harley Street specialist:

My Dear Greville,

I see a great deal of your good folks here. Indeed, they simply overpower me with kindness. Perhaps you've heard of the Theatri-cals last Monday and Wednesday. To see and hear your mother and Mrs. Godwin [Greville's Aunt Charlotte] on the stage was an experience I shall never forget. I offered to engage both for a

London Season and saw my way towards making a fortune, but alas! the sprightly young things [Louisa was 76, Charlotte 81!] did not jump at it . . .

Your dear father looks splendid so far as his face is concerned . . . I think he likes having me here. I give him all my stale Savage Club jokes, and it does one good to hear him laugh. Then he enjoys my songs so much and it's such a privilege to talk to him and hear his beautiful ideas of life and its responsibilities . . .[28]

Nicoll's remarks about George MacDonald are unconsciously patronising. It is clear that the old man is no longer the active head of the clan, but a declining figure to be humoured, conjectured about and listened to—with some reverence, perhaps, but mainly with tolerant amusement.

The gradual increase in eczema and insomnia together brought MacDonald's intellectual life to a close. When his old friend Carey Davies died just before Easter, he wrote to comfort his widow, but writing even a letter was by now a great effort for him:

I have been indeed unable to think, and still more to know what I am thinking. Indeed I feel sometimes as if I were to lose all power of thought. But when I find Carey again, he will help to set me right.[29]

This was in fact the last letter MacDonald wrote, though he sometimes added a line to one penned by Louisa. His decline accelerated that year as the eczema became much worse, until by the autumn he was driven almost out of his mind. He was aware of his mental state, and it distressed him more than the torment of his itching skin. Louisa described his misery in a letter to Greville:

Suddenly Father exclaimed, 'They say, don't they, my wits are all gone?' 'No,' I said, 'the wits are out in the back premises at present. We all know that.' Then that despairing look came into his face: 'I know you are all going away from me and I'm going to be left in a strange house.' . . . I with my arms round him told him *I* should never leave him and that Irene [his eldest surviving daughter] and I loved nothing in the world so much as to be with him . . . He really is not worse, only I think, not having you, it seems worse for him and for us . . .

159

> I asked him if he'd like Irene to sing, and so she did ... It was
> perfectly lovely to see his face transform from the intensely
> unhappy creature to the wondering, listening, loving soul that
> shone out of him at the very beginning of her 'O Salutaris'. 'Beauti-
> ful, beautiful,' he exclaimed. All through it she sang so
> humanizingly—gently. So now we are hoping much from music.[30]

She continued to write regular accounts of his progress, how in
November his nights were much better, and that one day he
suddenly remarked 'There's nothing but *Amore*' and then 'I
shall never see Greville again—Oh! my boy, my Greville.'[31]
He was becoming increasingly taciturn, and his pain from the
eczema grew even worse. Louisa had to employ professional
nurses to help with the task of looking after him.

Then in 1899 he suffered a minor stroke. His eczema
cleared, he was able to sleep, and he was no longer troubled by
the loss of his wits. His blue eyes were as keen as ever, and he
seemed to his family always to have an air of expectancy. He
spoke hardly a word in the next five years, and was looked
after as a semi-invalid.

It was clear to the MacDonald children that their father and
mother must come home to England. Robert, an architect,
drew up plans for the building of a house in Haslemere, West
Sussex. Greville wrote in a letter for his father's 75th birthday,

> Yesterday I signed the contract for the building of St George's
> Wood. For that, an' it please you, will be your English Home for all
> your earthly time. Bob's plans are quite perfect, I think; and there
> you will easily gather together in your arms—you and Mother—
> all your children. It should be a lovely home, set among huge
> beech-trees.[32]

In the summer of 1900 they installed George and Louisa in
their last home. Greville actually owned the property, and
gave his mother the lease of it at a rent of one shilling a year.
'That first rent still remains among my treasures', he wrote
years later, 'in its little ornate box where my mother humor-
ously and securely packed it for me.'[33] Though she could still
find room and time for humour, Louisa worried over George's
continuing silence, and over her own mental powers, now failing likewise. Greville wrote to comfort her,

160

Picture 6. MacDonald the visionary and mystic. His role as the Evangelist in *The Pilgrim's Progress* aptly expressed these qualities, well captured in this photograph by his son Robert. (*Photo: MacDonald-Troup Collection*)

Picture 7. George and Louisa MacDonald with Irene. This photograph was taken in 1901, presumably at 'St George's Wood' Haslemere. Louisa died six months later. (*Photo: MacDonald-Troup
Collection*)

'He to whom the Eternal Word speaks' said Thomas à Kempis, 'is set at liberty from a multitude of opinions.' And I often think Father in this his day of silence may be listening, perhaps in the dreamland of his Novalis, for the Eternal Word. Anyhow he is resting free from the 'multitude of opinions' which do but chatter irresponsibly . . .

Don't trouble, dear Mother, about your failing memory. It is only asleep, waiting till Sunrise sweeps away the shadows. Like the other sense-organs—eyes, ears and tongue—it too waits deliverance.[34]

On 8 June 1901—not the actual date, but the one most convenient for all the family to gather together—they celebrated at St. George's Wood Louisa and George's golden wedding anniversary. Greville had taken lessons from a goldsmith so that he could make a fifty-link gold chain for his mother.

In its clasp I set a star-sapphire, my father's favourite stone, to be symbolic of his uniting indisseverably that half-century of years. At intervals on the chain I hung eleven various stones, each separately set, to suggest the characteristics of each child: the four already gone denoted by flawless pearls.[35]

Octavia Hill wrote warmly to Greville about the special event, remembering the years she had been associated with the Mac-Donalds:

. . . It is delightful to me to think of those wonderful old days in your parents' house, Bude and its breakwaters, Hammersmith and the garden and the river and all the sweet and high converse of the good and wise in which you all grew up, and in which we who had the high privilege of their friendship shared; and to think we are now united in such a lasting work. What a light those days have thrown forward, so that now when physical strength wanes, the might of love remains royally triumphing.

What a gathering the Golden Wedding must have been, such a weight of memories, such a well of love that would tax even your mother's strength; but the blessing of all your love would be about them both.[36]

This letter must have been particularly gratifying to Greville, for during the last few years of the nineteenth century he had

had to face the painful fact that his father was outliving his popularity. Not that George MacDonald himself cared; by this time he was beyond such worldly considerations. But Greville was conscious that times were changing, that the public was less interested in questions of theology, that his father's mystical approach was already seeming quaint and out-of-date. To the people of Haslemere, for example, George MacDonald was not the man with a deeply-felt, heaven-inspired message of hope and love, but only the rather lovely old man with the long white beard, who could be seen in summer taking his daily drive dressed in a red cloak, white serge suit and grey felt hat. It was good for Greville to have Octavia's reminder that his parents had touched, influenced and stimulated many other lives during their fifty years' pilgrimage; and that the spiritual gifts they had given were still remembered with love and gratitude.

Louisa's health began to deteriorate rapidly after the Golden Wedding celebrations. She was worn out with nursing her husband, and began to suffer a great deal of pain. She could eat hardly anything. Yet her main thought was to conceal her condition from George. Night-times were most difficult, for they still shared the same bed; but she managed on the whole to do without the night-nurse's help and so kept her husband in ignorance. George himself was in no pain, and seemed to be sunk in a state of sweet senility:

> He gave no anxiety, enjoyed being read to, but almost never spoke. Yet it troubled my mother that he seemed to be in less constant need of her. I think she never realized his lively watching for her return, whenever she was absent.[37]

Louisa still managed to write loving letters to her children. In September 1901 she sat down to write to Greville, and included this little message:

> 'I'm writing to Greville', I said to Father; 'have you any message for him, dear?'
> 'Yes' (pause, I coaxing him; then) 'Yes' (pause again; and then quite softly) 'My interminable love!'

Of the letter, Greville wrote 'This is the last direct message I ever had from my father. It will surely last me for the duration of time.'[38] It was his mother who died first, however, in January 1902. She was buried at Bordighera, with the bodies of her children. Winifred and Irene were looking after their father. For several days they dared not tell him that his beloved wife was dead. They were not even sure how much he would understand of his loss. When they did at last tell him, he wept bitterly.

Winifred had married Edward Troup in 1897; now she took her father to live with her at Ashstead, Surrey. Irene came too, and nursed him devotedly until her marriage in 1904. 'He was always waiting, always beautiful to behold ...' writes Greville. 'If anyone came to the door ... he would turn and look with a moment's quiet expectation, and then, seeing it was not my mother, would sigh deeply and begin his waiting again. He was keeping the long vigil till she came for him.'[39]

He died, aged 80, on 18 September 1905. His body was cremated and the ashes buried at Bordighera with the body of Louisa.

> The darkness thinned; I saw a thing below
> Like sheeted corpse, a knot at head and feet.
> Slow climb the sun the mountains of the dead,
> And looked upon the world: the silence broke!
> A blinding struggle! then the thunderous beat
> Of great exulting pinions stroke on stroke!
> And from that world a mighty angel fled.[40]

The works of George MacDonald

Most of MacDonald's published works are listed here. Dates refer to first publication in book form in the UK.

1855 *Within and Without*   Longmans
1857 *Poems*   Longmans
1858 *Phantastes*   Smith, Elder & Co
1863 *David Elginbrod*   3 vols. Hurst & Blackett
1864 *The Portent*   Smith, Elder & Co
     Adela Cathcart   3 vols. Hurst & Blackett
1865 *Alec Forbes of Howglen*   3 vols. Hurst & Blackett
1867 *Annals of a Quiet Neighbourhood*   3 vols. Hurst & Blackett
     Dealings with the Fairies   Strahan
     The Disciple, and Other Poems   Strahan
     Unspoken Sermons, First Series   Strahan
1868 *Guild Court*   3 vols. Hurst & Blackett
     Robert Falconer   3 vols. Hurst & Blackett
     The Wow o' Rivven   Strahan
     The Seaboard Parish   3 vols. Tinsley Bros.
1870 *The Miracles of Our Lord*   Strahan
1871 *At the Back of the North Wind*   Strahan
     Ranald Bannerman's Boyhood   Strahan
     Works of Fancy and Imagination   10 vols. Chatto & Windus
1872 *The Princess and the Goblin*   Strahan
     The Vicar's Daughter   3 vols. Tinsley Bros
     Wilfrid Cumbermede   3 vols. Hurst & Blackett
1873 *The History of Gutta Percha Willie*   Henry King
1874 *England's Antiphon*   Macmillan
1875 *Malcolm*   3 vols. Henry King
     The Wise Woman   Strahan
1876 *Thomas Wingfold, Curate*   3 vols. Hurst & Blackett
     St George and St Michael   3 vols. Henry King
     Exotics [translations of German & Italian verse]   Strahan
1877 *The Marquis of Lossie*   3 vols. Hurst & Blackett

166

1879   *Sir Gibbie*   3 vols. Hurst & Blackett
         Paul Faber, Surgeon   3 vols. Hurst & Blackett
1880   *A Book of Strife, in the Form of The Diary of an Old Soul*
         Privately
1881   *Mary Marston*   3 vols. Sampson Low
1882   *Castle Warlock*   3 vols. Sampson Low
         Weighed and Wanting   3 vols. Sampson Low
         The Gifts of the Christ Child   2 vols. Sampson Low
         Adela Cathcart, revised edition   Sampson Low
         Orts   Sampson Low
1883   *Donal Grant*   3 vols. Kegan Paul
         A Threefold Cord   Privately
         The Princess and Curdie   Chatto & Windus
1885   *The Tragedie of Hamlet, A study*   Longmans
         Unspoken Sermons, Second Series   Longmans
1886   *What's Mine's Mine*   3 vols. Kegan Paul
1887   *Home Again*   Kegan Paul
1888   *The Elect Lady*   Kegan Paul
1889   *Unspoken Sermons*, Third Series   Longmans
1890   *A Rough Shaking*   Blackie
1891   *There and Back*   3 vols. Kegan Paul
         The Flight of the Shadow   Kegan Paul
         A Cabinet of Gems [poems by Sir Philip Sidney]   Elliot Stock
1892   *The Hope of the Gospel*   Ward, Lock
1893   *Heather and Snow*   2 vols. Chatto & Windus
         Poetical Works   2 vols. Chatto & Windus
         A Dish of Orts   Sampson Low
1895   *Lilith*   Chatto & Windus
1897   *Salted with Fire*   Hurst & Blackett

Notes and references

MacDonald's works exist in many different editions. To assist the reader who wishes to track quotations to their source I have added chapter as well as page number where appropriate.

Introduction

1. Sir William Geddes in *Blackwoods Magazine*, quoted in George MacDonald's obituary notice, *The Times*, 19 September 1905.
2. From 'Death and Birth', *Poetical Works*, Chatto & Windus, 1893, Vol. II, p. 24.
3. Greville MacDonald, *George MacDonald and his Wife*, George Allen & Unwin, 1924, p. 2.
4. Ronald MacDonald, 'George MacDonald: A Personal Note', *From a Northern Window*, Nisbet & Co., 1911.

Chapter 1

1. 'A Sketch of Individual Development', *A Dish of Orts*, Sampson Low, 1895, p. 43.
2. *George MacDonald and his Wife*, p. 32.
3. *Ranald Bannerman's Boyhood*, Blackie & Son [1886], Ch. II, p. 7.
4. *Alec Forbes of Howglen*, Hurst & Blackett, n.d., Ch. XII, p. 41.
5. *Ranald Bannerman's Boyhood*, Ch. XXI, p. 162.
6. Ibid., Ch. IX, p. 50.
7. *George MacDonald and his Wife*, p. 35.
8. *Ranald Bannerman's Boyhood*, Ch. III, p. 15.
9. *Poetical Works*, Vol. I, p. 134.
10. *George MacDonald and his Wife*, p. 59.
11. *Ranald Bannerman's Boyhood*, Ch. XXX, p. 244.
12. *George MacDonald and his Wife*, p. 64.
13. Ibid., p. 53
14. Ibid., pp. 36, 37.

Notes and references

Chapter 2

1. *Robert Falconer*, Cassell & Co., 1927, Part II, Ch. V, p. 189.
2. *The Portent*, quoted in *George MacDonald and his Wife*, p. 73 and footnote.
3. *George MacDonald and his Wife*, p. 78.
4. Ibid., p. 80.
5. Ibid., p. 81.
6. Ibid., pp. 92, 93.
7. Ibid.
8. Ibid., p. 99.
9. Ibid., pp. 105, 106.
10. Ibid., p. 103
11. Greville MacDonald, *Reminiscences of a Specialist*, Allen and Unwin 1932, p. 13.
12. *George MacDonald and his Wife*, p. 94.
13. Ibid., p. 95.
14. Ibid., p. 110.
15. Ibid., p. 108.
16. Ibid., p. 111.
17. James Matheson's daughter Annie, poetess and friend of Greville MacDonald, wrote the entry on George MacDonald in the *Dictionary of National Biography*.
18. *George MacDonald and his Wife*, p. 120.
19. For details of Scott as preacher and lecturer, see Edward Fiddes, *Chapters in the History of Owens College and Manchester University, 1851–1914*, Manchester University Press, 1937.
20. *George MacDonald and his Wife*, p. 128.
21. Ibid., p. 125.
22. Ibid., p. 127.
23. Ibid., pp. 120, 121.
24. Ibid., pp. 129, 130.
25. Ibid., p. 131.

Chapter 3

1. *George MacDonald and his Wife*, p. 137.
2. See also Stephen Prickett, 'The Two Worlds of George MacDonald', *North Wind*, No. 2, 1983, pp. 14–23.
3. *George MacDonald and his Wife*, pp. 137, 138.
4. Ibid., p. 138.
5. Ibid., p. 142.
6. Ibid., p. 140.
7. Ibid., p. 146.

8. *Within and Without, Poetical Works*, Vol. I, p. 2.
9. Ibid., p. 80.
10. *George MacDonald and his Wife*, p. 150.
11. Ibid., p. 155.
12. *Annals of a Quiet Neighbourhood*, Strahan & Co. [1880], Ch. I, p. 13.
13. *George MacDonald and his Wife*, p. 158.
14. *Reminiscences of a Specialist*, p. 350.
15. *George MacDonald and his Wife*, p. 169.
16. Ibid., p. 171.
17. Ibid., p. 172.
18. Ibid., pp. 185, 186.
19. Ibid., p. 179.
20. Ibid., p. 180.
21. Ibid.

Chapter 4
1. *George MacDonald and his Wife*, p. 193.
2. Ibid., p. 197.
3. *The Seaboard Parish*, Kegan Paul [1884], Ch XV, pp. 170, 171.
4. *George MacDonald and his Wife*, p. 185.
5. Ibid., p. 203.
6. Ibid., p. 204.
7. *Mary Marston*, Sampson Low, 1881, Ch. LVII, p. 355.
8. *George MacDonald and his Wife*, p. 213.
9. Ibid., p. 230.
10. Ibid., p. 235.
11. Ibid., p. 244.
12. Ibid.
13. Ibid., p. 247.
14. Ibid., p. 249.
15. For an analysis of the Byron marriage, see G. Wilson Knight, *Lord Byron's Marriage*, Routledge & Kegan Paul, 1957.
16. *George MacDonald and his Wife*, p. 251.
17. Ibid., p. 157.
18. Ibid., p. 254.
19. Ibid.
20. Ibid., p. 262.

Chapter 5
1. *George MacDonald and his Wife*, p. 270.
2. Ibid., p. 271.

3. Ibid., pp. 272, 273.
4. *Reminiscences of a Specialist*, p. 14.
5. *George MacDonald and his Wife*, p. 278
6. Ibid., pp. 280, 281.
7. Ibid., p. 282.
8. Ibid., p. 281.
9. Ibid., pp. 286, 287.
10. *Reminiscences of a Specialist*, p. 28.
11. *George MacDonald and his Wife*, p. 289.
12. Ibid., p. 290.
13. Ibid., pp. 290, 291.
14. 'A Hidden Life', *Poetical Works*, Vol. I, p. 167.
15. *George MacDonald and his Wife*, p. 294.
16. Ibid., p. 295.
17. *The Seaboard Parish*, Ch. XXXVI, p. 505.
18. *George MacDonald and his Wife*, p. 296.
19. *Phantastes*, Arthur Fifield, 1905, Ch. XIII, p. 172. In some editions Chapter XIII is in two parts, and this sentence is given as the superscription to the Conclusion of Chapter XIII.
20. Ibid., Ch. XIII, p. 154.
21. Ronald MacDonald, 'George MacDonald: A Personal Note'.

Chapter 6
1. *George MacDonald and his Wife*, p. 300, footnote.
2. *Poetical Works*, Vol. I, p. 441.
3. Republished as *Stephen Archer and Other Tales*, Sampson Low, 1883. I assume the title 'The Gifts of the Child Christ' to be an early misprint. Greville MacDonald catalogues it as 'The Gifts of the Christ Child', and throughout the story itself MacDonald always refers to the 'Christ Child' and 'the gifts of the Christ Child'.
4. *George MacDonald and his Wife*, p. 312.
5. Ibid., p. 318.
6. Ibid., p. 313.
7. Ibid., p. 318.
8. *Reminiscences of a Specialist*, p. 107.
9. See Raphael Shaberman, 'George MacDonald and Lewis Carroll', *North Wind*, No. 1, 1982, pp. 10–30.
10. *David Elginbrod*, Hurst & Blackett [1871], Part I, Ch. XI, p. 52.
11. *George MacDonald and his Wife*, p. 323.
12. *Reminiscences of a Specialist*, p. 15.
13. See David Holbrook, 'George MacDonald and Dreams of the

Other World', *SEVEN*, Vol. 4 1983, pp. 27–37; and my reply, 'Worlds Apart', in *SEVEN*, Vol. 5 1984, pp. 26–33.

14. *The Vicar's Daughter*, Edwin Dalton, 1908, Ch. XXXVII, pp. 301, 302.
15. *Reminiscences of a Specialist*, p. 27.
16. *George MacDonald and his Wife*, pp. 347, 348.
17. *Wilfrid Cumbermede*, Kegan Paul, 1891, Ch. XV, p. 136.
18. *George MacDonald and his Wife*, p. 356.
19. Ibid., p. 358.
20. Ibid., p. 149.
21. *What's Mine's Mine*, Kegan Paul [1886], Ch. XXIX, p. 212.
22. Joseph Johnson, *George MacDonald, A Biographical and Critical Appreciation*, Isaac Pitman & Sons, 1906.
23. *George MacDonald and his Wife*, p. 472.
24. Ibid., p. 337.
25. *Annals of a Quiet Neighbourhood*, Ch. XIV, pp. 300, 301.
26. *George MacDonald and his Wife*, p. 362.
27. *Reminiscences of a Specialist*, p. 43.

Chapter 7
1. *George MacDonald and his Wife*, p. 385.
2. Ibid., p. 381.
3. Ibid., p. 383.
4. See my article, 'The Poverty of Riches', *North Wind*, No. 1, 1982, pp. 31–9.
5. *Annals of a Quiet Neighbourhood*, Ch. XI, p. 196.
6. *Mary Marston*, Ch. XXXIX, p. 232.
7. *Robert Falconer*, Part III, Ch. VIII, pp. 379, 380.
8. *Reminiscences of a Specialist*, pp. 41, 42.
9. *George MacDonald and his Wife*, p. 392.
10. Ibid., p. 396.
11. Quoted in *George MacDonald, A Biographical and Critical Appreciation*.
12. *George MacDonald and his Wife*, p. 412.
13. 'George MacDonald: A Personal Note'.
14. *George MacDonald and his Wife*, p. 399.
15. *David Elginbrod*, Part III, Ch. XII, p. 333.
16. *Thomas Wingfold, Curate*, Kegan Paul, 1887, Ch. XIX, p. 92.
17. *George MacDonald and his Wife*, p. 412.
18. *The Princess and the Goblin*, Penguin 1964, Ch. 22, p. 155.
19. Ibid., Ch. 25, p. 173.

Notes and references

Chapter 8

1. *Reminiscences of a Specialist*, p. 108.
2. Ibid., p. 100
3. *George MacDonald and his Wife*, p. 417.
4. Rose probably died from *anorexia nervosa*. See Joan Abse's biography, *John Ruskin, the Passionate Moralist*, Quartet Books, 1980.
5. *George MacDonald and his Wife*, p. 384.
6. Ibid., p. 422.
7. Ibid., p. 423, footnote.
8. Ibid., p. 424.
9. *At the Back of the North Wind*, Blackie & Son [1886], Ch. XXXV, p. 353.
10. *George MacDonald and his Wife*, pp. 428, 429.
11. Reprinted in George MacDonald Society Newsletter No 2, September 1981
12. *George MacDonald and his Wife*, p. 429.
13. Ibid.
14. Ibid., p. 430.
15. Ibid., p. 438.
16. Ibid., p. 441.
17. Reprinted in George MacDonald Society Newsletter No. 2, September 1981.
18. *George MacDonald and his Wife*, p. 445.
19. Ibid., p. 451.
20. Ibid., p. 452.
21. Ibid., p. 456.
22. Ibid., pp. 459, 460.
23. Ibid., p. 461.
24. *Reminiscences of a Specialist*, p. 47.
25. Ibid., p. 48.

Chapter 9

1. Ronald MacDonald, 'George MacDonald: A Personal Note'.
2. *Paul Faber, Surgeon*, Chatto & Windus 1883, Ch. XIII, p. 82.
3. Ronald MacDonald, 'George MacDonald: A Personal Note'.
4. Bernard's son, Dick MacDonald, followed in his father's footsteps; he died in 1984 after a distinguished career in the Canadian theatre.
5. *George MacDonald and his Wife*, p. 471.
6. Ibid., p. 472, footnote.
7. Ibid., p. 480.
8. Ibid., p. 479.

9. Ibid., p. 388.
10. Ibid., p. 491.
11. Ibid., p. 489.
12. *A Book of Strife, in the Form of a Diary of an Old Soul* (reprinted in *Rampolli*, Longmans 1897) November 3rd.
13. C. S. Lewis, Preface, *George MacDonald: An Anthology*, Macmillan 1946, p. 21. See the article by Glenn Edward Sadler, 'Defining Death as 'More Life': Unpublished Letters by George MacDonald', *North Wind*, No. 3, 1984, pp. 4–18.
14. *Diary of an Old Soul*, January 9th.
15. Ibid., September 26th, 27th.
16. Quoted by Sadler, op. cit.
17. *Sir Gibbie*, Hurst & Blackett [1880], Ch. VIII, p. 43.
18. *Reminiscences of a Specialist*, p. 182.
19. *Paul Faber, Surgeon*, Ch. XXVII, p. 229.
20. *George MacDonald and his Wife*, p. 490.
21. *The Seaboard Parish*, Ch XXXIV, pp. 482, 483.
22. *George MacDonald and his Wife*, p. 505.
23. *Reminiscences of a Specialist*, p. 178.
24. *George MacDonald and his Wife*, p. 508.
25. Ibid., p. 530.
26. 'A Christmas Carol', *Poetical Works*, Vol. I, p. 299.
27. Op. cit., Vol. II, p. 132.
28. Op. cit., Vol. I, pp. 251, 252.
29. Op. cit., Vol. II, pp 95–98.
30. *Reminiscences of a Specialist*, p. 200.
31. Ibid., p. 208.

Chapter 10
1. *The Tragedie of Hamlet, a Study*, Arthur Fifield, 1905, p. 277.
2. *George MacDonald and his Wife*, p. 509.
3. Ibid.
4. Ibid., p. 511.
5. Ibid., p. 532.
6. Ibid., p. 513.
7. Ibid., p. 515.
8. Preface to *For the Right*, Karl Emil Franzos. English translation Julie Sutter, 1887.
9. V. A. Thisted, *Letter from Hell*. English translation by L.W.J.S., Bentley & Son, 1889. Preface, p. viii.
10. *George MacDonald and his Wife*, p. 518.

11. Letter from Francis Troup to James MacDonald Troup. *North Wind*, No. 4, 1985.
12. *George MacDonald and his Wife*, p. 521.
13. Ibid., p. 524.
14. Ibid., p. 525.
15. Ibid., p. 526.
16. *Reminiscences of a Specialist*, pp. 311, 312.
17. *George MacDonald and his Wife*, p. 539.
18. *Reminiscences of a Specialist*, p. 312.
19. *Heather and Snow*, Chatto & Windus, 1893, Ch. XIV, p. 105.
20. *George MacDonald and his Wife*, p. 542.
21. 'To an Autograph-Hunter', *A Threefold Cord, Poetical Works*, Vol. II, pp. 290, 291.
22. *Lilith*, Chatto & Windus, 1895, Ch. XLIII, p. 324.
23. Ibid., Ch. XLVII, p. 350.
24. Ibid., p. 351.
25. *Reminiscences of a Specialist*, p. 320.
26. Ibid., p. 321.
27. Ibid., p. 331.
28. Ibid., p. 284.
29. *George MacDonald and his Wife*, p. 545.
30. *Reminiscences of a Specialist*, p. 335.
31. Ibid., p. 336.
32. Ibid., p. 342.
33. Ibid., p. 346.
34. Ibid., p. 347.
35. Ibid., p. 349.
36. Ibid., p. 95.
37. Ibid., p. 351.
38. Ibid., p. 354.
39. *George MacDonald and his Wife*, p. 562.
40. 'The Chrysalis', *A Book of Sonnets, Poetical Works*, Vol. I, pp. 265, 266.

Select bibliography

The Victorian Background

Abse, J. *John Ruskin—the Passionate Moralist*. Quartet Books, 1980.

Avery, G. *Nineteenth Century Children*. Hodder & Stoughton, 1965.

Backstrom *Christian Socialism and Co-operation in Victorian England*. Croom Helm, 1974.

Burton, E. *The Early Victorians at Home*. Longman 1972.

Chadwick, O. *The Victorian Church*. A & C Black, 1966.

Christensen, T. *Origin and History of Christian Socialism, 1848–54*. Acta Theologica Danica Vol. III, Universitetsforlaget I Aarhus, 1962.

Drummond, A. L. & Bulloch, J. *The Scottish Church 1688–1843*. St Andrew Press, Edinburgh, 1973.

Fiddes, E. *Chapters in the History of Owens College and Manchester University 1851–1914*. Manchester University Press, 1937.

Knight, G. W. *Lord Byron's Marriage*. Routledge & Kegan Paul, 1957.

Maurice, F. D. *The Kingdom of Christ*, ed. Alec Vidler. SCM Press, 1958.

Nicholls, M. *Some Trends in Theological Education in London 1830–1890*. Unpublished, 1981.

Tuke, M. J. *A History of Bedford College for Women 1849–1937*. Oxford University Press, 1939.

About George MacDonald

Johnson, J. *George MacDonald, a Biographical and Critical Appreciation*. Isaac Pitman & Sons Ltd., 1906. Reprinted Haskell House Publishers (USA) 1982.

MacDonald, R. 'George MacDonald: A Personal Note', *From a Northern Window*, Nisbet & Co., 1911.

MacDonald, G. *George MacDonald and his Wife*. George Allen & Unwin, 1924 Reprinted Johnson Reprint Corporation (USA). *Reminiscences of a Specialist*. Allen & Unwin, 1932.

Troup, E. 'Notes on George MacDonald's Boyhood in Huntly', *The Deeside Field*, 1925.

Bulloch, J. M. 'A Centennial Bibliography of George MacDonald', *Aberdeen University Library Bulletin*, Vol. V, No. 30, February 1925.

Select bibliography

Escott, H. *God's Troubadour: The Devotional Verse of George MacDonald* [anthology]. Wayside Books, Epworth Press, 1940.

Lewis, C. S. *George MacDonald: an Anthology*. Macmillan, 1946, Fount paperback, 1983.

Sadler, G. E. *The Cosmic Vision: A Study of the Poetry of George MacDonald*. Unpublished thesis, 1966.

Reis, R. H. *George MacDonald*. Twayne Publishers, New York, 1972.

Hein, R. *The Harmony Within*: The Spiritual Vision of George MacDonald. Eerdmans, Grand Rapids, Michigan, 1982.

Triggs, K. *George MacDonald: the Seeking Heart*. Pickering & Inglis, 1984.

Journals relating to MacDonald studies

North Wind, Journal of the George MacDonald Society (The Library, King's College, London).

SEVEN, An Anglo-American literary review, published by Wheaton College, Illinois, USA.

Inklings, Organ of the Inklings-Gesellschaft für Literatur und Ästhetik (Erster Rote-Haag-Weg 31, D-5100 Aachen).

Index

Acknowledgements

I would like to thank my friends in the George MacDonald Society for assistance, hospitality and encouragement; the staff of Bradford Central Library for patient and courteous help with my researches; Camera Press for the picture of John Ruskin on p. 111; Tony D Triggs for his critical insights; and Mrs F Leyson for permission to reproduce photographs from the MacDonald-Troup Collection.

K. T.
November 1985